# THE GORGEOUS REVOLUTION

## Our Doorway to Sovereignty

# Foreword

I wrote this book nearly seven years ago. In fact it literally wrote itself during three days in a hotel room. Back then, I didn't quite know what to do with it, but persisted in pursuing publishers, some of whom were very intrigued, but who just didn't commit. I shelved it two years ago, wondering what would become of it.

Biding my time.

So here we are, June 2017, and the green lights have turned on. The timing is right. The big picture is being revealed and now I understand 'the wait'. We are ready now. My six decades on this earth have prepared me well for what is to come.

Our Doorway to Sovereignty is now beckoning. Sovereignty, quite simply explained by the Oxford Dictionary is 'a self-governing state'. Well, I'll have that please. To be at the effect of no one, to call my own shots, to follow the deep inner calling only I can hear. And to have the courage to follow that voice, decisively.

So, without further delay, I invite you to join me, and let our Gorgeous Revolution reveal herself in all her glory.

Postscript: Feel free to highlight, mark notes in margins, and stamp your own story on these pages. Pick out the eye teeth, trawl and dig deep. Make this your Revolution too.

And visit us at **www.gorgeousrevolution.com** to stay in touch.

# Introduction

**If you have picked up this book, then you are curious, for this is a book like no other.**

It calls for radical change in a world where such change can make you radically uncomfortable.

It runs counter to the monolithic global beauty tide.
I'm not going to gloss. Too many in the self-help industry make life look so easy.

Well, it is, and it isn't.

And you read those books, give it a go, and then fall off the wagon to go searching for something new.

**I'm here to tell you there is nothing new.**

What if you couldn't be fixed, made better than, made whole, or enlightened.

**What if there was never anything wrong with you?**

Ever.

And all you had to do was open your eyes to what is already there.

Right now.

And stop searching for what you have been, all along.

I am writing this book because I have a sense of urgency.

Things must change and change soon. The planet is not

well. And many of us are not well.

I am writing this book because I can't see people unhappy with their bodies any more.

It hurts me to see young women want new breasts because they don't like the ones they have.

It hurts me to see fathers of young women lament as they see their daughters crave a different shape.

It hurts me to see women constantly battling with food, good food, bad food, and starving and purging themselves.

Secretly.

It hurts me to see women push their partners away because they don't like their own thighs.

And it hurts me to see so much money and angst spent in getting hair right.

It hurts me to see such amazing creative energy get funnelled into competing, all life long. For what? A place in the beauty queue? A moment in the sun when someone else thinks we're pretty enough to matter?

I want women, young and old, to be free.

To be their own unique beauty. To let the sun shine through.

To be themselves. Gloriously.

Without a beauty poinl of vicw.

To be able to tune their radar to what they are really here to do.

Contribute to the world by being all they can be, and more, and more.

**To be as BIG as they truly be.**

## So, I'd like to invite you to...

Imagine a world where everyone is happy.

Everyone knows exactly what brings them joy, and that is what they do.

Everyone knows exactly how they contribute to life itself.

They know what they are here for.

Some love cooking, some teaching, some stocking shelves, working with numbers, designing vehicles, designing clothes, setting up systems, making pies, blowing glass, assembling computers, selling cars, designing houses, building bridges, making roads, caring for cows, singing, dancing, kicking balls, growing vegetables, body boarding waves, making face creams, leading countries, telling stories, writing books, acting in films, grooming dogs, birthing babies and detailing dirty cars and more.

Imagine all have found their place in a big jigsaw puzzle, spinning through space, and all is well. Because they are happy, really happy. There is no illness, communities care for each other with inclusion and kindness, there is no crime, all are nourished, there is music, art, beauty, laughter, kindness, rich cultures, thriving fields, flowering rooftop gardens, and no fighting.

Anywhere.

And all are blossoming, beyond compare.

What if every one of the seven and a half billion people all worked together in harmony? Corporations share their wealth, care for team members' health, clean rivers flow easily, energy is generated freely, and the news channels are all good news, interesting, inspiring educational good news.

Imagine if we could just live like that for just one day.

Even just your neighbourhood, even just your street, even just your family, or even just one person.

You.

Because change starts with you.

Just you.

As we are all connected, you change you, and we change the whole.

So listen up now.

**You are that crucial to the world.**

## CONTENTS

Chapters:

| | | |
|---|---|---|
| 1. | Puppy fat. What puppy fat? | 11 |
| 2. | What if there was never anything wrong with you? | 15 |
| 3. | The Truth about Your Body. | 17 |
| 4. | Guilt stifles Life. | 19 |
| 5. | Throw your scales down the garbage shute. Now | 21 |
| 6. | I dare you. Just ask your body. | 23 |
| 7. | Me, Myself and Ego. | 28 |
| 8. | The Dreaded Lump. | 30 |
| 9. | So what if it was no longer about YOU? | 33 |
| 10. | How can I expand my life today? | 35 |
| 11. | We must look LOVELY. | 38 |
| 12. | Our judgements stick us, like glue. | 41 |
| 13. | What if we live as pure Possibility? | 43 |
| 14. | And what if everything is just your Perception? | 45 |
| 15. | What if your Body could be the Leader in your life? | 48 |
| 16. | You are here to be Uniquely Different. Be free to be it. | 50 |
| 17. | What if everything is not necessarily what it seems to be? | 52 |
| 18. | Problem. So I am a spy who thinks she is Jesus. | 55 |
| 19. | But just WHO is doing the choosing? | 57 |
| 20. | For we are all connected. | 60 |
| 21. | And is this really Mine? | 62 |
| 22. | Why, oh why, are relationships so hard? | 65 |

| | | |
|---|---|---|
| 23. | Marriage. Let the chains come off, honey. | 66 |
| 24. | From the cozy, warm bed. To the icy, raging torrent. | 70 |
| 25. | When in deep water, become a diver. | 71 |
| 26. | Who says nice girls can't get angry. Just watch me. | 72 |
| 27. | When the jug is cracked, the water spills from it. | 74 |
| 28. | Gratitude is not a fluffy word. It is a deep, sacred state of being. | 78 |
| 29. | Anger. So what if it was really your potency? | 81 |
| 30. | The Potency of Singularity. | 83 |
| 31. | A few things my husband taught me about men. | 88 |
| 32. | Receive. Receive. Receive. | 91 |
| 33. | And a few things about family my children taught me. | 94 |
| 34. | My daughter and me. | 100 |
| 35. | Teenage Postscript: A request by our son. | 102 |
| 36. | It takes time to compete. Appointments all week. | 104 |
| 37. | Let's start Our Revolution. Right Now. | 108 |
| 38. | Food is Great. | 110 |
| 39. | Our Revolution continues. Have more sex. Fullstop. | 114 |
| 40. | Sexuality and Sensuality. The difference will set you free. | 118 |
| 41. | The Little Black Dress and God. | 123 |
| 42. | Menopause. Bring it on. | 128 |
| 43. | The Beauty Cocktail. Are you drunk enough yet? | 132 |
| 44. | The Future does look rosy. | 141 |
| 45. | Generation G. | 148 |
| 46. | Begin It Now. | 157 |

# Before we get started

This is not a beauty book.

Nor is it not a book about self-esteem.

Nor is it a book about 'spiritual enlightenment'.

You may notice I do not have angels on the cover, nor purple. Anywhere.

This is not a book about how 'amazing, awesome, phenomenal, beautiful, transformed, goooooorgeous, enlightened and extraordinary' you are.

Pink syrupy, hypnotic language of the New Age kind just lulls us into thinking we are so 'transformationally connected', that all we have to do is go ooohh, ahhh, and look into each other's eyes and all will be well.

It won't.

When you leave the workshop, it won't. When you get back to the daily grind of life, it doesn't change.

Your guru just left town.

All the crystals, metaphysical healings, readings, chanting, white light and sharing goddess circles won't change a thing.

**Unless you choose.**

In a world where it is OK for twenty something year olds to have botox, and breast implants, I wonder where we lost ourselves. Maybe in the search to be the fittest, the sleekest, the glossiest, the smoothest, the firmest, the plumpest, the most buffed, the most gelled, the most manicured, hair straightened, accepted and cosmically cool, we simply lost the plot.

Our bodies are simply commodities. Our houses are too big, our lifestyles too credit card extended, out plasma screens too many.

And our shoes too bizarre.

And we are dying. From cancers, broken hearts, and depression induced ailments.

Just like our planet.

So, we require nothing short of a Revolution. Where we tip it all upside down, look at it from an entirely different perspective, take a deep breath, and simply ask...

## Who are we REALLY and why, oh why, are we here?

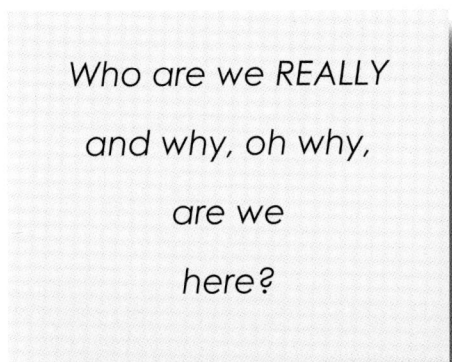

*Who are we REALLY and why, oh why, are we here?*

So this is a book about you. **The Bigger You**. It is a gutsy, pragmatic, simple look at the truth.

I said I don't do gloss. I don't do sweet very well either.

I do do provocation. And I do tell the truth. And the truth is sexy. Very sexy.

It is vibrant, full, luscious, evocative, and gloriously available. To us all.

### If you choose

As Marianne Williamson wrote for Mandela...

"Our deepest fear is not that we are inadequate. Our deepest fear is that we are powerful beyond measure. It is our **light**, not our darkness that frightens us.

We ask ourselves, who am I to be brilliant, **gorgeous**, talented, and fabulous?

### Actually, who are you not to be?"

You don't write a book. It writes you. It tells you when it is ready. Now is the time.

**We are starting a Revolution.**

**Our Gorgeous Revolution.**

**Because something has to give.**

It is a book about true beauty, acceptance, and potency beyond what we have ever considered before, and it is a book about taking action.

By the time you have read it you will never look at your body, nor anyone else's, the same way again.

And your life will change.

Together with your relationships. Your health. Your wealth. Your plans.

I cannot NOT write this book. It has called to me, provocatively, for years, and I am now compelled to act.

## We have just gone too far.

## Chapter One:

## Puppy fat. What puppy fat?

I was born a chubby, bubbly, happy child.

We lived in a middle-class way. I was oblivious to my chubbiness except when my ballet leotards bubbled from my middle when I tied my pink crossover. But I could jump really high, so I thought I was good. And my pink tutu twirled in the light of the mirror. To me, I was beautiful. Unquestionably beautiful.

I sparkled.

One day my Dad, who adored me, as Dads do, said, 'Won't it be great when you lose your puppy fat'.

**Puppy fat...what puppy fat?**

I started a diet the next day, and continued it for twenty three years. Even after he died when I was only twelve.

You might ask why? I have pondered that often, but I realise that I simply wanted to be special. Not ordinary, but special. And to please him. And losing weight, and keeping it off was the best way I could keep being special. To him, to anyone, to me. Everyone would notice me, like me, and listen to me.

That way I was different. But was acceptably different.
Specially different.

Yep. A major twenty three year divergence, but not an exclusive one.

For, I am not alone.

The majority of us diet. And strive for perfection. Some for years, and years, just like me.

## So what has dieting, or the ceasing of it, got to do with turning around the Titanic?

Everything.

We women remain small because of it. It consumes us. It always sits there at the back of our mind. And we fear being fat. And out of control. And aging. And being passed over. And if we are overweight, we are just that, out of control.

Dieting sits at the centre of dumbing down, controlling and fitting in. It prevents intimacy, vulnerability, questioning, true feeling, languid lusciousness, and freedom. We are prisoners in our own manicured, glossy, lipsticked, smooth underweared world.

The Divine cannot be heard in the body of a dieter, nor that of a serial botox user.

And when God cannot be heard, neither are we.

And when the body is no longer listened to, neither is the planet.

I remember being fourteen and secretly borrowing my mother's panty girdle. My newly found, robust curves were wayward, unacceptable, and I had to control them.

Years later, I remember trying to hide my steadfast panty girdle from my new lover, I just knew he would find it a turn off, so I hid it way at the back of my cupboard. I just pretended he didn't know I wore it.

Like the emperor's new clothes, I acted as if my body was always this perfectly sprung. It had to be. It must be.

Or life itself would not be worth it.

But now the Beauty Arsenal has made it easy. Support to be perfect includes not only dieting and botox, but also the incessant preening, smoothing, cutting, pumping, liposuctioning, ironing, lasering, bleaching, dying, straightening, spray tanning, polishing and injecting of our bodies.

**Because we are led to believe by an authoritative beauty industry we are special.**

**Chosen. Worth it.**

It took radical action to allow me to stop. It took questioning, counselling, money, and out on the edge searching to finally let go.

> *Because we are led to believe by an authoritative beauty industry we are special.*
>
> *Chosen. Worth it.*

Of never being enough.

And it took the adoration, the care and the patience of a partner who steadfastly believed I was beautiful, to chip away at my doubt and for me to one day walk free.

**Naked. Without any props, just me. Gorgeous me.**

**Well...wake up now.**

**We don't have the luxury of the time I had. I indulged myself.**

**We don't have another twenty three years to stop the madness.**

**It has to stop now.**

**We have to be all we are and more. And fast.**

**Now I could make this wonderfully tricky.**

I could take you down a path of spiritual teachers as long as your arm. I could read you your astrology chart, rebirth you, reiki you. I could tell you where your inner child was hurt, where your parents did a rotten job, where you are really a reincarnated goddess, a witch, a monk, or a princess. I could tell you it is going to take you ten cathartic sessions before you will feel anything.
I could tell you that you will suffer for your karma, your debts, your light, your zealous religious beliefs and satanic acts of a former life.

Well, I'm going to simplify it all for you, and just remind you of what you deeply, somewhere, already know. If I can distil a lifetime of reading, searching, personal developing, painful releasing and torturous group sharing, I will.

**Because we don't have another twenty three years.**

So, what if I simply asked…

## Chapter Two:

# What if there was never anything wrong with you?

For all my adult life I have explored ME. I have sought to make me better.

**Which of course implies there is something wrong with me in the first place.**

I have paid thousands of dollars to explore my inner landscape to FIX myself. Somehow be brighter, stronger, faster, more informed, more improved, than most.

Again, be special. But endless pursuits to be better have lead me back to the beginning, to the simple truth. And I ask again,

### What if there was never anything wrong with you?

*What if there was never anything wrong with you?*

What if every small niggly thing you have ever believed about yourself is a lie?

And what if, right now, I give you permission, full sanction, to be ALL you are and more? More please. More of everything you have tried to squash, forever.

What if none of your story was true?

And what if being 'out of control' was just that, BEYOND the control of others. FREE!

What if there really was only NOW?

Who would you be if you were not your body?

Who would you be if you simply let the charade drop now, the past drop now, and walked free?

No drama, no pain, no regrets, no judgement, no apology, no guilt, no niceness, no waiting...no excuse.

How BIG would you truly be then?

And how small have you been playing now, for FAR TOO long?

*Liberate your points of view.*

Well, here we go. Get on the train. Hold on, listen up, and get ready to **liberate your points of view**.

**Because our world, our very future, depends on it.**

## Chapter Three:

# The Truth about Your Body.

You do not fit inside your body. It fits inside you.

Your bigger you, the one that you get glimpses of between the breaths, is HUGE.

**You ARE the universe.**

And before you think I've gone mad, I'll prove it. Close your eyes.
Put your hands up, nearly touching each other, and feel the energy between them.
Just feel it. It exists outside your body too.

And as we know from science, energy knows no bounds, it continues.

> And our bodies are the transmitters of this energy.
> They are our cat's whiskers.
> Our wiring system, our way of receiving and transmitting information and energy.
> Of being AWARE.
> Of being connected.

Just as space does. So, therefore, we are really limitless. As big as the Universe in fact. Unlimited. Connected. We are in fact, ONE.

Now if we are ONE, then we share the same global possibilities, the same global mind, and definitely the same planet.

The Universe is, in fact, full of energy. Full of potential. Possibility.

**And our bodies are the transmitters of this energy.**

**They are our cat's whiskers. Our wiring system, our way of receiving and transmitting information and energy. Of being AWARE. Of being connected.**

Our body sees around corners. It knows what is behind the closed door when your small you does not.

Without our bodies, we do not experience.

We do not receive who we really are (because remember we ARE energy itself), so we have no way of experiencing pleasure, nor joy, nor love.

Our bodies are vehicles of pleasure, intuition, vibrancy, aliveness, joy and gratitude.

**And, at this current point in time, our bodies are way more aware than the small we, we pretend to be.**

They can repair themselves. Function on automatic, without interference. They multitask, create and generate, give pleasure, receive pleasure, see beauty, feel warmth, touch lightly, taste delicacies, dig dirt, caress babies, build cities, climb mountains, cry tears and sashay in frocks. They wear Laboutins with ease and catch footballs with grace.

Without them, we are not truly here.

**So why, oh why do we torture them, poison them, control them, overfeed, hate and berate them so much?**

**Why do we make them sick, cut them, truss them in tight underwear, starve them, drag them around and judge them?**

**All lifelong.**

## Chapter Four:

# Guilt stifles Life.

The very first meal I had after I finally stopped twenty three years' of dieting, was the most memorable of my life.

*For twenty three years I had eaten with guilt.*

Two poached eggs on toast on a plate.

They were like sweet breasts, gently wobbling with delight.
They tasted DIVINE.
I savoured every mouthful. Slowly.
And I was satisfied.

Satiated for the first time in years.

**For twenty three years I had eaten with guilt.**

The first time I ordered in a cafe with my new found freedom, I ordered an apple cinnamon scroll. And a hot chocolate.
Not a fake skinny hot chocolate.

Real milk.

Now, this was nearly three decades ago, and I still remember the pleasure I received from that warm pastry and that hot, nourishing drink.

I fed myself **and was present with myself** for the first time since a child.

## For Guilt stifles Life.

Guilty pleasure...what is that? Marketers get us to 'sin' by eating certain foods, to hide our pleasure...to eat alone. To make our guilty delights private.

Are we supposed to then go to confession because we ate an ice cream with a caramel filling?

I must have been so sacrosanct. So pure.

To never divulge from my stoical path of counting calories. Like a nun, I steadfastly held to my calorie counting while the rest of the world had fun. Then when no one was looking, I scoffed chocolate elephants (yes, you know THOSE Belgian hazelnut filled chocolate giant jumbos!) and then felt GUILTY for days . Oh, the shame of it all.

Then fuelled with renewed righteous piety, I would write out a new diet plan, and stick it on the back of the pantry cupboard. Roped in, I was in control again. And all was good.

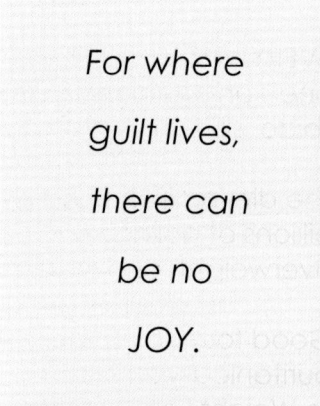

*For where guilt lives, there can be no JOY.*

I wasn't living. I was lurching from Monday to Monday stumbling to stay on the high ground, and secretly dying to live. Sound familiar?

To shed this secrecy, to literally come into the light and stay there has been the biggest most powerful, single challenge and gift I have ever given myself.

**For where guilt lives, there can be no JOY.**

## Chapter Five:

## Throw your scales down the garbage shute. Now.

EVERYWHERE I go there are diets. Everyone is on one. Be it a 'healthy one', one to lose weight, one to gain weight, one to energise your libido, slim your thighs, flatten your stomach, get virile, or stay young.

The dieting industry, including wellness fads, is worth billions and billions of dollars. And yet we are all confused. We remain overweight, and in fact, are getting bigger.

Good food, bad food. Naughty, indulgent or being good. Even puritanically saintly. Food does it all to us. It rules the roost. Welcome to Weight Loss Information Overload, or when all else fails, eat from a sachet for six weeks.

Oh yum.

Diets just don't work. The statistics show most people regain the weight, and just keep getting fatter.

And more malnourished. And more frustrated. And more depressed.

And weighing yourself every day is an addiction worthy of LOUD mention.

**I used to weigh myself every day. Sometimes twice, three times a day.**

It was either a good day or a bad day based on what the scales said. My whole sense of worth was measured in that single act. And if I didn't like the reading, I would try and cheat it, by leaning to the left or right or balancing on one foot.

Then one day, I snapped. I acted bravely. We lived on the 13th floor at the time, and I walked to the garbage shute and opened the door, and let them drop. From a big height, they tumbled down, crashing with a resounding metal thump.

I don't know what I weigh anymore.

I used to know exactly. I could tell you how much I weighed at every mile stone in my life. My first job, my second job, my first wedding, my divorce, my first pregnancy, all of it. A daily mental log.

Now somehow it doesn't matter anymore. It no longer matters at all. I get the feeling that if I did weigh myself, my body would double the amount, just to make an 'in my face statement'. Who REALLY cares!

*Perhaps we are dead anyway if our lives depend on the scale reading.*

It won't make me a better person, give me more love, make me special, make me happy or fill my heart. It won't complete me. Or win me Lotto.

Do you know some studies say people would rather be dead than fat?

## Perhaps we are dead anyway if our lives depend on the scale reading.

My body doesn't want to be weighed and measured. I know that now.

I asked it.

## Chapter Six:

# I dare you. Just ask your body.

**Consider this. Yep, a radical departure, I know, but play with me here.**

**Just what if we asked our bodies for a change....**

>what they want to eat?
>what they want to wear?
>where they want to live?
>where they want to work?
>how they want to move?
>Who they want to have sex with?
>what shoes they like?
>what partner is nourishing and caring to them?
>what waves give them the best ride?
>what holiday would be the most beneficial?
>what medicine, or vitamins, to take, or not?
>which accountant to go to?
>which business venture to choose?
>which house to invest in?
>which chiropractor to visit?
>which party to go to?
>which leader to vote for?
>what skin care to use?
>what lipstick to apply?
>what plastic surgery, IF AT ALL, it requires?

Yes, just ask your body.

**What if the answer to ALL your stressful, struggling choices could be as simple as ditching it all, and ASKING your body what IT wants?**

Think of the money you could save, (particularly those expensive scales that tell you your BMI as well!), the unfulfilled relationships you could avoid, the sale returns you could delete, the wardrobe mistakes you would never make, the hangovers you could never have, the waves you could ride, the JOY you could have.

## The approval you would never seek.

The 'knowingness' that would permeate every fibre of your being with certainty that eliminated fear.

The **TRUST** you would have in you.

**For you to be the source of all for you.**

## So, what if you always knew?

*For my body knows more than me.*

**What if all of life was chosen, without a point of view, by the BIGGER YOU, the one your body talks to?**

The one YOU never do.

Well, it is simple. That simple.

**Your body knows. Just ask it for heaven's sake. It has been sitting there, right under your nose for a lifetime, and you have never consulted it once**

**And neither had I.**

## For my body knows more than me.

Ever watched bodies walking? No two are the same. They carry their life stories in their shoulders, their hips, their tummies, their knees.

We store our hurts and pains in convenient out of the way places.

File, store, upload, and ignore. Until the pain gets too much. Then take a pain killer and soldier on. With stoical martyrdom.

**So stop now, stand still and BE PRESENT.**

**In the moment.**

Silent.

Just you and your body.

First of all, acknowledge your body. Touch it lightly. Talk to it. Thank it for being there for all these years, no matter what.

Show it some gratitude. Like a faithful hound, it will respond and wag its tail eagerly.

Then, when you are ready,

## Ask it a Question.

How will it answer?

Always correctly. Just remember to get out of its way.

**This is the bit that set me free. You see, IT IS NOT ABOUT YOU.**

**The little you who fights for control just went out the window.**

**RELINQUISH CONTROL. JUST DO IT NOW.**

Yes...ask it a question. Just do it.

You can take your time if you like. But give it a go.

Stand up, put you heels together, close your eyes, take a breath, and **ASK YOUR BODY** a simple yes/no question. Remember, you will be surprised at its capacity to respond.

**Body, do you want to eat this?**

**Yes or No**

**It will lean forward for yes, and back for no. Just lightly. Just subtly.**

You may get a slight tingling down your spine for no, or a warmth in your heart for yes. You will know. But you are going to have to be still, unhurried, to **LISTEN**, and feel.

**To connect.**

And your small self may not LIKE the answer. For it comes from a place you might not yet know.

**Body, do you want to wear this dress? Yes/No.**

**Body, will this purchase add to my life? Yes/No**

**Body, is this the accountant my business needs? Yes/No**

**Body, will it be nourishing to have sex with this person Yes/No**

**Body, will listening to this person on You Tube add to my life? Yes/No**

*This ONE tool will set you free from dieting for the rest of your life..*

**This ONE tool will set you free from dieting for the rest of your life.**

Ask your body what IT wants to eat.

You might be surprised.

And some of you will know what I'm talking about. For when we were pregnant and had those 'cravings', it was simply the baby's body yelling at us. It required that particular food to grow at that particular time. So our bodies told us what we HAD to eat. As a simple matter of life and death.

In my first pregnancy, my husband had to drive all over a large city to find me globe artichokes. I then ate tomatoes on toast at every meal for one week. During my second pregnancy, at the six week mark, I had such a meat craving I thought I was going to pass out.
I literally cried with an ache for meat. When it arrived, I scoffed the lot. Then turned off meat for two months.

I was vibrantly well through both pregnancies and had two healthy babies.

We'll listen to our babies' growing bodies, but why not ours?

Ah, for we are wayward, guilty and we need controlling.

Reining in.

To live freely would give us too much pleasure.

You see, bodies are really made for pleasure, not pain.

**PAIN is the domain of the Ego.**

## Chapter Seven:

# Me, Myself and Ego.

Thank you Eckhart Tolle and others for explaining Ego to me. I got it. So did my body.

I'll keep this as short as I can.

**Your ego defines you. The Small You.**

> *Your ego makes judgements. It wants you to be safe.*
> *To fit in. To measure up.*
> *To compete, to win, to own, to succeed, to be right. It must, above all, be RIGHT.*

**As the Bigger You is**
**indefinable, way bigger than you ever imagined, your ego can't control it.**

**Your ego is simply a part of you which you thought you required.**

**That keeps you safe and in control of your Small Life. And helps you fit in.**

Your ego buys your house, controls your body, your teenagers, your choice of car, your job, your brand choice (yes, particularly your brand choice), your diet, your school choice for your children, your haircut, your partner, your time frame, your 'lifestyle', your 'enlightened way in the world', your desires, your regrets, your resentments, your anger, your rage, your pain, your choice of groovy coffee, sunglasses or pantyhose. Or child's name. Or birthday party for that matter.

**Your ego makes judgements. It wants you to be safe. To fit in.**
**To measure up. To compete, to win, to own, to succeed, to be right.**
**It must, above all, be RIGHT.**

To never give in.

**The ego requires a lot of energy to be right.**

And when it has to be right ALL the time, it overrides all other choices, including the body.

Remember, the body operates through questioning, and accessing universal energetic wavelengths. Awareness

It operates way beyond control. When we let it.

When left to its own devices, it resonates with constant change, it can adapt, it can rebalance, reassess, let go, morph, change shape, **transmit light.**

The ego is not light. It operates on fixed points of view. It wants to win, not lose, succeed, not fail, control, not surrender.

When the ego is in continual control of the body, the body gets sick. It is as simple as that.

That simple.

How does it do that? **The ego judges.** Judgements, or old thought patterns, now considered by science to be energy too, stick the body.

So it has no way of showing up but as THAT.

We are, after all, just a BUNCH OF MOLECULES held together by a whole lot of thought patterns. Just energy.

I'm too fat, too thin, too wrinkly, too stupid, too different, too dark, not special, very special. I'm lonely, bereft, angry, resentful and right. And of course, too old. I'm sick, I hate you, I hate my breasts, I hate being a woman, it's dangerous being a woman, I'm over giving, I give too much, I hate my thighs, they are wobbly, less than, too big, not right. I'm a fighter. I'm so tired.

Never, ever good enough. Not worthy of love.

Worthless.

So the **ego CREATES its own truth.** The body sticks the judgements and shows up fat, thin, old and sick. And tired.

See, the **ego was RIGHT.**

## Chapter Eight:

## The Dreaded Lump.

Some years ago I developed a lump. A dreaded lump. My thyroid was seriously swollen. I had tests and scans and got called back in for more. I was losing weight rapidly, and not sleeping. I did my own investigations and was feeling less than happy. Palpable concern started to permeate my secret Dr Google searches.

I was struggling with my business, trying to make it happen. Everywhere was a dead end. I was a rat on the wheel but determined to keep going. My ego was in control. I stored every NO I received in the daily course of running my business in my throat and pushed on. Such a nice girl, I heard them say.

When, oh when, would it be my turn?

I returned to my wise naturopath, whom I had not seen for a while as I was so busy making things happen, and juggling adversity. She looked at me quietly and said I had a choice. I could go the regular route of surgery, or get busy. Writing.

She took a proforma from her desk, on how to write a forgiveness letter. She told me to go home and write a letter, using the proforma, to everyone I thought had ever 'let me down' in my entire life.

**So I did. When you think your life depends on something, you just do it.**

The list was long.

My Big Self took charge. I looked at my wounded ego fair and square in the face.

I sat it down in the corner, and I just wrote. Convincingly.

**From the heart.**

I forgave, not only them but me, for all the times I had belittled myself for failing and never getting it right. And for never speaking up. For being a Good Girl.

I not only forgave them, I was **GRATEFUL** for the experience. For the opportunity to choose something different. To expand.

Well, every day the lump got smaller. And every day I got a little lighter.

It took three weeks.

When I returned to the doctor a month later for something else, she was horrified to see I had refused more treatments. I showed her the lump has gone.

She did not believe me. She got angry, said I was incorrect and that they should test to check. Funny, I remember even now feeling a slight sensation of pain and lump return, even as I sat in her office. My body was picking up her fear and taking it on as its own. Her ego was strong. I must be wrong.

I left. I thanked her for her concern and left.

I have not to this day had a return of the lump. My ego has quietened. I am much less at the effect of others, I have learnt to ask a question and am guided by my awareness.

And when I forget who I am, and struggle with my lot, I remind myself that it is no longer up to me. For I let go

Impatience ceases to be when you follow internal instructions because we're actually not in charge of the timing. Tapping feet, grinding teeth and blaming others will not make it happen any quicker.

I cannot discuss this with a friend who works in a specialised medical field. In her eyes, I am highly irresponsible. I could not be right, because of her medical model. She could not have spent the majority of her life working with her patients and have healing happen that fast without authoritative research, medicine, machines, money, and expertise.

The medical model can be an example of ego. It has the scientific answers. It tells us what to do. But have you ever noticed that doctors look like some of the most unwell people on the planet?
For they too are simply human; often exhausted, over worked and over-qualified to change direction.

So what if that too could change? What if they too could see the world with a different point of view?

For all of us to see the whole.

Health and healing is a continuum. Some choose extreme intervention, and some choose a natural, inner reflective approach. Both are right, and both are wrong.

And there are egos at each end of the spectrum. It's a tricky path to tread when we give our power away.

What we can do is listen to our bodies more. Take responsibility for our emotions, our work choices and the food we eat. The feelings we digest.

And not look to the medical model to fix us all the time.

I wonder how the world might look then if we took the time to listen?

To ask our bodies a question.

And I wonder how our bodies might show up then, freely, **without a point of view?**

Maybe, just maybe, we would all be well.

We could see that illness is simply another choice.

We could all function optimally as consciousness designed, and maybe we could all get on with what we are all here to do.

When we choose.

## Chapter Nine:

# So what if it was no longer about YOU?

If we put ego in the corner with a blanket, a book, and a box of chocolates, and let **OUR AWARENESS** take the lead, our bodies would know what to eat, would hum with joy, would access pleasure, would cooperate, never harm, would care, nourish, nurture, dance, sing, resonate with wellness, be stress free, pain free, would age less, would radiate light and would access and transmit new energies available right now, as we evolve.

Our bodies, our hands, feet, brains, mouths, tongues, eyes, and hearts, would become the very instruments of the evolving, co-creating consciousness we truly are. As ever moving fractals, we could push the boundaries of what is possible here on this planet.

**We would truly, if we listened, together bring Heaven to Earth.**

**So, what if it was NO LONGER about you?**

What if you are now just a body with a sticky note with your name on it in fluro biro?

What if you were one with all, and could let the egos off the hook?

**Do you GET how GOOD that would feel?**

**If you were free?**

What if you were here at this time simply to be an instrument for change? To co-create with choice and awareness? What if all you had to do was get out of your own way and ask the question:

## How can I be of service today?

**How can I add to the world today? How can I propel change from a larger place?**

**Where do I have to go, who do I have to meet, and what clothes do I wear for my body to feel vital, expansive, and full of energy?**

## For it's NOT ABOUT YOU.

## And when you get that, EVERY SINGLE THING changes.

YOU can't MAKE it happen anymore. Your little ego is out of a job.

And so, my friend, is mine.

So we can't compete any more. We can't win any more, and we can't have 'the power over' any more.

## We can just contribute. To life itself.

And Consciousness, God, Divine Love, The Universe, whatever you want to call it, is generous beyond what we ourselves could ever imagine. When we align with that, all manner of synchronistic things happen without effort, without stress.

We sleep, we relax, we let go.

> *For it's NOT ABOUT YOU.*
>
> *And when you get that, EVERY SINGLE THING changes.*

## Because it is NO LONGER UP TO US TO 'MAKE IT HAPPEN'.

**Now if you get that bit, that alone will set you free for the rest of your life. Forever.**

Ah...breathe on that one for a moment.

Yes, I said **FOREVER.**

## Chapter Ten:

# How can I expand my life today?

Now, if you hold that question, and ALLOW yourself to see yourself doing the things you love that energise you, you will be told.

In pictures, words, phone calls, and just feelings. Exhilarating feelings.

Goosebumps work too.

### For you are here to be of service. YOU have a job to do.

And that job will expand you, it will ask more of you, it will utilise your talents in the most ingenious of ways so that it just doesn't feel like work at all.

Remember, your job is to do the things that bring you joy. Pleasure. Along with the other seven and a half billion of us. And as each one of us wakes up, we'll get on with it. Ask:

*For you are here to be of service. YOU have a job to do.*

**How can I expand my life today?**

And then wait. Be willing to do whatever it takes, without a point of view, and get on with your life and it will come to you.

**Your heart's desire.**

The one that only you know about.
That is buried somewhere deep.
Or shouts at you every day! That sweet spot where time stands still.

It is THAT simple.

(My job, well, at the moment is to write this book. I'm not writing it, I'm just using my fingers to type it. And having a ripper of a fun time doing it...sip of wine here...who said it had to be hard? The funny thing is, I knew I was going to write a book, not just when. I was told at 1 am this morning that I have three days to write it, so here I am in a suddenly booked hotel room, writing, just writing because that is what is necessary. And it feels so easy).

## It's NOT about you or me anymore. We can no longer MAKE it happen.

## We must listen now. With internal ears, our bodies, our knowing.

Imagine you are setting up a business. Remember, it is not about you.

Let the business talk to you. It has consciousness too.

Ask it questions like **"How can I serve you today?"**

Every component of that business will come to you, all at the right time, if you just ask.

Be specific however, and do what is required. Ask, do you need a business plan? If you get a yes, then do it. Ask your body to give you feedback all the time to make sure **you are working with awareness and NOT your EGO. Nor someone else's.**

Lying in bed and visualising it to happen just doesn't cut it. Get in there, roll up your sleeves, be prepared to do whatever it takes.

Evolving consciousness requires us to ACT.

**But to act with Awareness.**

**And to sometimes make a radical departure from how others do it.**

Ego will try to skip back in, especially when you fear. Or when others doubt your big plans, or when you have to 'prove' yourself to someone else.

So are we getting the hang of the Ego?

For most of us, it has had us by the short and curlies for way too long.

We have been driven to succeed, to be noticed, to get it right, to be enough in a society that is never satiated.

**It's time to act differently now. As Ghandi said, "Be the change you want to see in the world."**

So, let's return to the world of beauty.

For nothing will truly change until we get this.

For this will challenge you to the hilt.

But I'm going there anyway.

## Chapter Eleven:

## We must look LOVELY.

As women, we want to look beautiful. We have made our survival depend on it.

Every magazine displays page after page of beautiful women, yes, as we know, all airbrushed to the hilt. But we don't care.

Following the Holy Grail, we stand, a glistening credit card in hand. We worship at the temple of department store hush and listen attentively to the lovely lady in the white coat. To honour the Hope in the White Gilded Jar. For our job is to conform, to shine, to erase those lines and lather that cream. To present our best selves as never before.

**For we must look lovely.**

We have to whiten our smile, straighten our teeth, and pouf that hair. We have to close those gaps, lift that cleavage, smooth those lines, pout those lips, laser those hands, tighten that neck, fill those cracks. Lift those eye lids, paralyse that forehead, and peel that skin.

**And look lovely.**

We have to gel those nails, toxic manicure weekly, bleach those curls, dye those greys, and wax those unwanted hairs. We have to tighten those thighs, strengthen those arms, lift those buttocks, flatten that stomach, find that core, lengthen that stride.

**And look lovely.**

We must agonise over our teenagers, referee toxic family arguments, pray that our children won't be beaten up at school, and pray that no one will know,

**And look lovely.**

We have to be moist and ever ready, meditate like a monk and have sex like a goddess. Be smart, ambitious, together, informed, connected, and on top. Smart phone on, IPad savvy, internet driven. But of course, we also must be there for the little children, sport a designer bag, cook like a chef, and jog with a Fit Bit.

**And look lovely.**

I don't know whether to laugh or cry having written that. I'm knackered.

## Houston, we have a problem.

The world is dying. And we dye our hair.

The earth is hurting, animals disappearing, the oceans are polluted, and we hate our thighs.

> *We have lost sight. We have become blind.*
>
> *To what matters, to life itself.*
>
> *To who we really are.*

Prisons are full, wars are raging, teens are suiciding, and we laser our lines.

Women are raped, old people homeless, forests destroyed and we don't like our breasts.

Children are starving, nations malnourished, and we are buying our next diet book.

Does something, anything, not make sense here?

## Am I really THAT alone, or am I the only one going mad here?

## Please stop. Take a breath and just stop. Please.

You see, our egos have us by the short and curlies yet again, as well as around the neck, and have chained us to our credit cards.

## We have lost sight. We have become blind.

## To what matters, to life itself.

## To who we really are.

Our egos want us to compete in a world of never-ending patent pending anti-wrinkle claims. Because it's fun, isn't it? And necessary. Otherwise, we'd be letting ourselves go. Letting ourselves down. Letting Team Woman down. And we wouldn't be special, wanted, accepted or worthy of love anymore.

So we are hooked. The commercial beauty world is happy, lipsticks sold, breasts uplifted and toes shiny red.

And the planet is dying.

**Body, oh body, is anybody listening?**

Here comes the crunch. The crux of the matter. Then if you don't agree with me after this, please put this book down for we are wasting each other's time.

We have two choices: **change or die.** That simple.

The changes we make now will determine whether we continue as a viable human race or not. And it does depend on us. So if the elevated evolution of the human race depends on us as its tools, then we had better listen up.

And start listening to our bodies.

For they are the bridge to a different life.

**For all on Earth.**

Let me explain.

## Chapter Twelve:

# Our judgements stick us like glue.

Judgements, that is, our daily thoughts, beliefs, and conclusions, create our reality here on earth.

*Every judgement you have about your body stops you being present in your life.*

Our collective judgements create our social norms. Our cultural experience.

And judgements stick in our bodies. They create stuck bits that cannot move,
nor change, nor transform. And what doesn't change, atrophies. Dies.

For change is the only constant in our universe. Try to control it, and you're out of here!

## So what if you could live your life with ease?

## No judgement? No set conclusions? No rigid points of view?

What if life itself was a giant fractal, with us well aware of the ride?

If you knew you were **THAT BIG** and lived from a place beyond compare, would you really care if you had a wrinkle or two, your teeth didn't sparkle, your thighs wobbled slightly?

## Every judgement you have about your body stops you being present in your life.

## Right now.

You can't HEAR what is really going on. The entire awe inspiring miracle of this universe is passing you by because you judge yourself for being five kilograms over weight?

I should know.

Let's return to my original question.

**SO WHAT IF THERE WAS NEVER ANYTHING WRONG WITH YOU?**

**If you were not your body, bigger than that, ETERNAL in fact?**

**How would you live your life then?**

Look at it now: your relationship, your finances, your body, your stresses, your failures, your problems, your pain, your hurts, your past, your debts, your betrayals, your indiscretions, your secrets?

**So I ask you, if you KNOW you are truly bigger than you, ask yourself:**

## Would my BIG ME really choose that?

If you have now closed the book, I wish you well. Happy journey.

If you are still with me, our work has just begun. Because you just chose something different. You just chose a different possibility.

## You just chose YOU.

Truth is **YOU ARE THAT BIG.** We all are.

Truth is our bodies are our cat's whiskers, our transmitters. Truth is, we are all there is.

And more.

One with the Universe, One with each other, One with the Planet.

If you are still with me, then breathe. Take a moment to rest.

Good. Now we're all on the same page, let's go.

## Chapter Thirteen:

# What if we live as pure Possibility?

We have reached a time in history where our future now depends on us NOT knowing all the answers. To be comfortable to not know form.

I know it sounds like I am contradicting myself. Well, sometimes knowing all the answers stuffs us up

To stay curious, in the question, creates change, possibility, and flow.

**When we think we know, we stop the flow of what is possible.**

**And to LIVE as the question means to live in a state of wonder.**

**Of all possibility.**

**Now THAT is surrender.**

**And I can tell you, it can hurt. Physically hurt. I did. Your mind will go nuts. It is trained to KNOW. To work things out. To fix things, solve things, and be clever.**

**But what if nothing was solvable?**

**What if there was nothing but change?**

So start feeling comfortable with your mind not knowing. Because all things change.

**And it is now not about you.**

Remember, you are just a bunch of molecules held together by your thoughts and points of view.

So am I. We are all in this together.

So if we suspend those points of view, our world can change.
We will be able to hear what our inner voice is telling us, and we will be able to act from a different, more connected, expanded place.

**For the good of ALL.**

## Chapter Fourteen:

# And what if everything is just your Perception?

I want you to play with me here. I want you to experiment.

## Again....What if everything is just that, your perception?

Your body. Your partner. Your mother. Your teenager. Your daughter. Your job. Your boss. Your debt. Your savings. Your desires. Your relationship. The media. The education system. Your bank manager. Your favourite TV programme. Your best friend. Your worst enemy. Beauty treatments. Lipsticks. Your wrinkles. Food. Money. Fame. Poverty. War. Cellulite, yes even cellulite.

**All just an interesting set of beliefs, you bought off the shelf.**

**And what if all of it could change, if we changed that point of view?**

**What if the way we PERCEIVE the world is the way we create it?**

**What if rigid PERCEPTION locks molecules in place to exude all else? And what if changing our PERCEPTION, changes our world?**

Just digest that one for a moment.

Quantum scientists will tell you the observer themselves affects the outcome...no person is an island unto themselves, we are all connected. So what if we ALL operated from awareness? From openness and possibility? What would our world look like then?

I wonder..... Now this, I know, is true.

My body knows more than my ego. My ego keeps me small. I have way more fun with others when I connect, and it is my ego that keeps me separate.

So, I now pledge to let my body be the leader on this earth plane, not my ego. In fact, mine just left the room.

Elvis Ego just left the room. Just not centre stage anymore.

**So I invite you to stop. Right now.**

**And be still.**

**Breathe.**

**Be the valley between your breaths.**

**And just be with your body. For it has been here all along.**

It has carried you from birth, been there every waking moment, washed cars, washed dishes, birthed babies, walked a million miles, rode buses, been pummelled, penetrated, caressed, bruised, poked, shoved, pushed, glared at, squeezed, drugged, boozed, stuffed, pilatesed, yogaed, triathloned, starved, and ignored.

Not once asked...**Body, what would you like for a change?**

So please read this poem, then put this book down and be with your body.

In stillness.

West Coast of Scotland near Oban: Steffen Boettcher

To Love yourself, start here:
Take your own hand – put it to your lips
then
lay the soft of your cheek, to the round of your shoulder
where
the faint musk
of enduring dreams and the labours of your life
perfume you.
It's a start.
It's a beginning.
Now the ache in your heart

*has*

*a*

*surface*

.

To Love Yourself -
© Em Claire

Now thank your body for leading you home.
Be the energy of **GRATITUDE** for its every breath.
Its every heartbeat.
Take as long as you like. I'll be here when you get back.

## Chapter Fifteen:

# What if your Body could be the Leader in your life?

Your body is all knowing, and connected to all there is when you simply get out of its way.

So from now on, just do this. Put it in the driver's seat. Let it be your chauffeur.

> *There is no money to be made by giving us back choice.*
>
> *To listen to our body and not the marketers' voice.*

Ask it a question...and then listen...it will tell you its secrets too. When you are ready.

Bodies are not wrong. There is nothing wrong with them. They can heal like that. They can grow back organs, skin, bones, and teeth. When allowed. They are magical. They can morph, they can bend, mend, open up, transmit joy.

They can also regenerate. Maybe that includes skin.

It is only our points of view that have solidified them. Our own limitations of what is possible.

Our points of view we have learnt from others. From education, magazines, marketers, beauty houses, parents, authority, girlfriends.

So what if for us to move forward, flexibility, an open, enquiring mind and a vibrant, connected, transmitting body were all that were needed?

Remember, most beauty marketers who say they can fix your body, implying that it's broken, really just want you to part with your money. Their bottom line is invariably more important than your true wellbeing.

**There is no money to be made by giving us back choice.**

**To listen to our body and not the marketers' voice.**

If we all really chose from a place of truth, the commercial world might fall apart. Not a bad thing. It means it might change its need for control and provide us with products that actually add to our lives, not keep us tied to our credit cards.

So before you buy another thing...ask.

Body, will this be nourishing?

Body, will this enhance my life?

Body, do you want to wear this?

**If your body leans back, put it back on the rack.**

**Ah, there is power now in being off the beauty grid. Off the consumer rat wheel.**

**For you now have CHOICE.**

## Chapter Sixteen:

## You are here to be Uniquely Different.

## Be free to be it.

Everyone is. There's a job for you that no one else can do. You are part of a big jigsaw puzzle.

You will know when you are on track when you feel light. When everything flows. Everywhere you hold a judgement of you or someone else is where you lose connection. Lose your way.

**We have lost our way in the beauty world.** Our bodies have become fodder for the marketers and an endless source of money for the greedy. And we have become lost, in a clever advertising maze, seeking purpose and satisfaction outside of us.

> *Because you will be part of the flow to bring Heaven to Earth.*
>
> *Yes, to bring Heaven to Earth.*

Instead of listening for the signs, the guidance for what you are really here to do.

**So, what are you really here to do? What will set you free?**

I recommend that before you dye your hair, take that gym class, botox that frown, suction those thighs, apply that toxic chemical on your skin or eat that diet food, you ask:

### Body, does this work for us?

The response you get might just amaze you.

And welcome you to a world of freedom you never knew existed. A new dimension, right under your nose.

And when you do that, your life will never be the same again.

**You are connected.**

If you ask a question without seeking an answer, you sense a new possibility. You have joined with the flow of the giant fractal, and you are on your way. Where to, I can't say. Other than it will be better than you ever imagined.

**Because you will be part of the flow to bring Heaven to Earth.**

## Yes, to bring Heaven to Earth.

## Chapter Seventeen:

## What if everything is not necessarily what it seems to be?

When I was little, I wanted to be a missionary. That was hit on the head real fast, so I replaced it with a vet. Then an architect, because my Dad was one. When I was fifteen, I lived in Japan as an exchange student. Remarkable place. I was completely at home. I remember crying when I visited the temples in Kyoto. I didn't know why. I just did.

I declared that, as my University days neared their end in the mid-seventies, I would do anything but teach. Anything. (Funny how we sometimes resist the very things we are here to do). I was a bright straight A student, but I knew I didn't want to be a doctor, a lawyer, a school teacher or an office worker. Funnily enough, ASIO, the national security Intelligence agency, heard of me via my mother's friend, and I joined them. I became an Intelligence Officer. I became a would-be spy.

Now the only reason I'm telling you this is that during my time as a would-be spy, a number of things happened, some of which you too may have experienced. It happens when you 'wake up'. Some people wake up fast, others slower. I was of the faster, freight train variety.

I was married. A lovely wedding, a lovely man. I was twenty three. I married for love. For two years, I cooked, sewed, darned socks, worked at being a spy, had dinner parties, ski holidays, and good times with friends. I was, for all intents and purposes, very happy.

**But everything is not necessarily what it seems to be.**

I was, in fact, so deeply unhappy it wasn't funny. And I didn't know why.

I had insomnia, I had to drink port wine at 3am to fall asleep on the lounge room floor. I tried really hard to be good. To fit in. To tell myself all was OK. My job was interesting, and I could put off having babies for a while.

Being a spy was great. I got to put all my talents, including my writing skills, and my love of leather skirts and drinking whisky to good use. I was bright, involved, well liked and intelligent. I had prospects.

**But, remember, everything is not necessarily what it seems to be.**

One day I broke all my own rules and went to lunch with a man who made me laugh. The rest is history. I left my husband some ten months later. If I had stayed with him, at the age of twenty five, I would have died inside.

Not his fault. A beautiful man, just not the one for me.

I tried to end the attraction. I tried to fight it. I tried to fit the mold, the wedding vows, the picket fence dream. But my body just couldn't do it anymore. I remember going to the other man's house, and telling him it was all over and I was going back to my husband. He listened. And just as I was leaving, he said these simple words:

*What does Deirdre's Deirdre want?*

That was your husband's Deirdre speaking...what does Deirdre's Deirdre want?

## What does Deirdre's Deirdre want?

For the first time in my life, I really broke all the rules.

**I chose for me, I chose ME.**

I was vilified, I was shunned, I was isolated, I was left out in the cold. My family disowned me. No one understood. No one could help, no one even knew what I was going through. How could they? I was a twenty-five year old liar, a cheat, and selfish.

But I was FREE.

**I could start my new life by choosing for me.**

**Years later, I remember reading somewhere that to be free one must be willing to betray another to not betray your own soul. I get that now.**

**I betrayed society's norm, my husband, my marriage vows and my family's wishes and reputation.**

**But I did not betray my own soul.**

Being true to your own soul invites rapid change, beyond our control.

A subsequent chain of events unfolded fast that somehow catapulted me somewhere, somewhere I have been looking for again, for the rest of my life.

## Chapter Eighteen:

## Problem. So I am a spy who thinks she is Jesus.

When I turned twenty seven, I met another man, and we fell in love. My whole world turned on its head, and suddenly I woke up one morning. In a head space, a place I had never known.

**I thought I was Jesus.**

Now please keep in mind that I was still an Intelligence Officer with ASIO, and certain security cautions apply when working in such a job. When I arrived that day hugging everyone, and telling them it was all going to be OK, the Powers That Be thought it required a visit to the in-house psychiatrist.

You can imagine a CIA operative thinking they are Jesus as ringing the odd alarm bell.

I was in a state of bliss, euphoria, happiness not known by many. So they assumed I was on drugs. I wasn't. I was just high on life itself, so connected to the Universe, and receiving constant downloads. In hindsight, Jesus was the only reference my mind could give me at the time (I had after all gone to a Church of England school) so I went with it. They wanted to medically placate me. I was obviously having a nervous breakdown of sorts and needed a rest.

So I refused the drugs and took a week off. It was the most compelling, intense week of my life.

I had moved in with this new man, and I think he was in a remarkable state too.

I hardly slept. I didn't need it. I wrote all night, wrote instructions for jobs that had to be done.

I glowed. I would sit on the balcony and be one with the stars. I literally was HUGE. I would get on a tram-car, and people would move away, like as if an unfamiliar energetic field prevented them from coming too close. I was connected to all, giving kind words everywhere, and the world seemed to move in slow motion, I felt it all, was aware of it all...and just KNEW it was all going to be OK.

It lasted nearly three weeks. I was like a balloon, flying high, but with people tugging at my string. Begging me to stop this, stop the stupidity, and come back to earth. Come back and be responsible. I was laughed at, and ridiculed by some, and was the source of curiosity and concern by others.

When I finally came 'back', it all fell apart. I listened to others and not to myself. I lost my connection.

Or so I thought.

But obviously, I had been imbued with something great.
A homeopathic reminder of who I really am.

As I mentioned, I was twenty seven at the time. At the time of writing, I am fifty four. It has taken me another twenty seven years to come home. To know who I really am. I have looked for nearly three decades to find that connection again. Courses, healings, parting with money, readings, fastings, journeys, purple, rainbows, more money, crystals, more courses, I searched.

Only to find myself again at the beginning.

Now I find my feet on the Earth, my heart in my hands, my body connected, and my plans at the ready.

I now no longer care what you think of me. I now know who I am.

**FOR WE ARE MUCH BIGGER THAN WE THINK WE ARE.**

And it may be this book will blow the cobwebs away, or simply give you permission to be your real you too.

Right now.

Because our future depends on it. We now must live the biggest lives we can. We must be the BIGGEST WE we can be.

**For we are bringing Heaven to Earth.**

**Chapter Nineteen:**

# But just WHO is doing the choosing?

I didn't realise just how foreign a concept 'choosing for me' was until I sat outside of it all and just watched.

Choosing for me could be considered egotistical. It could be considered selfish, unprincipled, stubborn and just plain wrong.

It upsets the equilibrium, the whole. The Mexican crabs have a job to do. Stick together or else.

In Japan, they have a saying: The nail that sticks up must be hammered down.

But in a world of self-satisfaction, instant gratification, tweets, Facebook, mobile phones, Instagram, instant credit, infinite choice...then I have a right to ALL the choices available...don't I?

If metaphysical gurus now tell me nothing is right and nothing is wrong, and there is only just now, then what is the problem with me having what I want?

Right now.

And if that doesn't work, then choose again. I can't make a mistake, right?

**Now the challenge with choice is quite sneaky. Just WHO is doing the choosing?**

**Your Ego or your Bigger You?**

**And nine times out of ten it is the Ego.**

Hence we have a world full of brands, cars, shoes, clothes, houses, mobile phones, lipsticks, moisturisers, eye creams, potential partners, holidays, jewellery, perfume, restaurants, food, furniture, cushions, magazines, internet sites, and we get to choose, based on how we define ourselves, and our cultural norms, what works for us.

So I'm going to pose something different here.

What if we only had just one choice?

**To ask our bodies.**

**Body, will this be expansive?**

And then have the courage to go with whatever comes up.

**The deeper response.**

Even if it is different to everyone else.

Even if it means you might leave your job, your partner, and everything you own.

Or not. Your body's choice.

> *What if there was such a grand order to life and the Universe itself that by being part of that, engaged with it, we could help bring about that order, magnificently?*

**What if there was such a grand order to life and the Universe itself that by being part of that, engaged with it, we could help bring about that order, magnificently?**

What if that is your purpose in life? Just that. To bring about that order by being engaged, asking questions, never assuming, and being attentive to nuances.

By being aware. **And following your heart's desire.**

**And having FUN, yes, operating from a lighter place. A more inclusive place.**

So what if EVERY time we chose ANYTHING, we asked first,

**Body, will this be expansive?**

As you get better at this, it starts to flow, doors open, and your world literally becomes light.

Choosing ANYTHING becomes easy. You ask your body. After a while you don't have to lean back or forward, you just get an instant answer. You know.

**And when you ask from this place, you are asking for the whole.**

## Chapter Twenty:

# For we are all connected

My awareness knows everything.
It knows if those sneakers were made in a sweat shop, it knows if that cream has a toxic substance for my body,
it knows if that lawyer is a crook.
It knows if that gorgeous hunk will turn out to be nasty, it knows if that food will make me sick, it knows if those shares will fall. Or rise. And if I fail to ask a simple question, and come from a conclusion based on what my Ego wants, so I can fit in and benefit, win or lose, then I am not connected to the whole.

*There is a bigger plan waiting for you than you ever imagined.*

I am small.

**So how many of YOUR choices do you make from Ego? Or from Fear?**

Your clothing, your laptop, your sex partners, your car, your job, your choice of words, your beauty routine, your temper?

Are they made from a place of guilt, persuasion, competition, envy, blame, abject fear or apathy? Are they even made for you? Or does everyone else choose for you and you just go along with it?

**There is a bigger plan waiting for you than you ever imagined.**

When you have the courage to choose for you, quietly, in the present moment, just for you.

You will be guided along a path to freedom, to expansion that sits right at your door.

If you dare open it.

For Universal Intelligence has a job for you, one only you can do. You have your own set of instructions. No one else's.

For your life is like no one else's.

**And so is your contribution.**

We may all HAVE different things, which from an egotistical standpoint, we can measure.

Some have more, some have less.

But our BIGGER SELVES are all equal. We are all One.

And when you live your life from that place, all competition ceases.

When you choose life as your Bigger You, your life, unfolds brilliantly, magically.

**Ask your body...just ask the question...and watch a myriad of false choices fall away. You will be left with that which is most rewarding for THE WHOLE.**

**And that includes YOU.**

## Chapter Twenty One:

## Is this really Mine?

If we are just energy, space and awareness, and all connected, then every thought, feeling and emotion we feel might not actually belong to us.

Ponder this.

You are feeling great. Happy, alive, it's going to be a good day. You walk into the kitchen, and you instantly feel your partner is not happy. They are in fact fuming. You pour your cup of tea, and your lightness starts to go. You read the newspaper. It's not a happy world. You begin to feel tired, heavy, you drag your feet out the door.

Your mother calls, she is having a bad day. It is only 8.30am, and when you awoke you felt great!

Now you feel like crap. It's going to be a long day.

So where did you go? What did you buy that wasn't yours?

**Maybe, just maybe, none of it is yours?**

**Maybe you just pick up thoughts from everyone else, make them your own, and then go about your day as if you have no choice.**

I heard of one woman who lost five kilograms just asking "Mine or someone else's?" every time she felt hungry at work. She would reach for a muffin, chocolate bar, or protein bar every time she detected hunger. Not once did she ask if it was HER hunger, her craving.

It wasn't.

For our minds can be like sponges if we let them. Sponges on 'automatic trawl'.

I used to suffer terribly from insomnia. Adrenals would be on overload, I would have panic attacks, feared trying to go to sleep, took

Valerian, St John's Wart, lavender, counted sheep, whatever, and none of it worked.

Until one day, some very observant aware person simply said when I asked about it:

> *Maybe you just pick up thoughts from everyone else, make them your own, and then go about your day as if you have no choice.*

**Is this really Mine?**

It never was. I had made it mine. It belonged to a family member.

And within ten seconds it had gone.

And I have not had a problem since.

So it made me question. Where else was I not choosing for me? And how many other 'perceptions' was I buying that weren't mine? So I looked at all the places that caused me angst in my life and realised that I was operating automatically, on someone else's wavelength.

- Fear of spiders: not mine.

- Fear of being fat: not mine.

- Fear of being left: not mine.

- Fear of poverty: not mine

- Fear of failing: not mine

- Fear of never being enough: not mine.

- Backache: not mine.

- Headache: not mine

- Craving: not mine (only pregnant women really understand that!)

Because, just like Chinese whispers or some pervasive STD, we pick it up, take it on, and pass it around. And never, ever stop to question:

## Is this really Mine?

**So, if we now turn all of this around, do you see how we can also affect the whole, in a positive way?**

**For if we pick up on every thought, feeling, and emotion, then for those of us who are aware, and KNOW we have choice, we can make a deliberate choice to be calm and happy. And those around us will feel better. And they in turn will help those around them feel better, and so it goes.**

**We can knowingly insinuate calm and happiness by simply BEING IT around others.**

To be kind, nurturing, smiling, caring for our bodies, considerate of ourselves, creative with our thoughts, expansive with our ideas, supportive with our plans, grateful with our hearts, and present with our actions, we might just infect the whole planet with a new way of thinking and being.

That too is possible!

So stick it on your computer, on your car steering wheel, on your bathroom mirror, on your forehead. Get your kids to remind you (and they will). I don't really care. But just ask 10, 20, 50, 100 times a day.

**Is this really mine? Is this mine or someone else's?**

And if it frees up at all...please **RETURN TO SENDER**....whoever that may be.

You might just discover your life gets a whole lot easier!

So now you are getting the hang of it, choose for your Bigger You, and the rubber begins to hit the road. We have progress. Life is getting better, well at least more interesting!

## Chapter Twenty Two:

# Why, oh why, are relationships so hard?

For lifetimes, many of us who have sought enlightenment probably lived like monks, in a cave, meditating, and not having much to do with others.

It's a cinch being enlightened in a cave.

> Consciousness is simply the willingness to be present in each moment, without judgement.

But when you throw in a twenty one year old marriage, teenagers, a business, suppliers, family, mortgages, afterschool sport, girlfriends, mothers-in-law, mothers, tuckshop duties, body maintenance, Twitter, Facebook, and 7.5 billion people on the planet, the cave seems a long, long way away.

## Consciousness is simply the willingness to be present in each moment, without judgement.

Savour that for a moment. Because that is all it is.

Nothing more. Nothing less.

**From there, you can be aware of all things, when you simply ask a question. It therefore follows that from that place you can choose what works for you.**

Great. What if my family don't like it, my husband is upset, my kids hate me, and my parents reject me?

If you are choosing from the place of Truth, that includes a place for all.

Let me invite you, and then you too can see what works for you.

## Chapter Twenty Three:

## Marriage. Let the chains come off, honey.

Most marriage vows don't take into account change. Most marriages start off well, get a bit soggy after a few years, get weighed down with mortgages, kids, aging parents, expectations, school fees, lost dreams, and average sex.

We just DO marriage. Just as our parents did. And if it didn't work, we get divorced.

Or have an affair.

The sparks, attraction, magnetism, everything we felt at the beginning gets lost, covered up, buried under a pile of stuff, ironing, bad situations, little hurts, turned backs and we wonder where it all went.

Some of us who are 'aware' choose to work on our marriage, clear our baggage, bring enlightenment to the situation, seek counselling, time apart, time together, and make it happen.

Meanwhile, our secretly harboured dreams are banging at the door, we are under the hammer, running out of time, wondering if we are getting enough, and hedging our bets. Just like rats in a maze, we too keep hoping that one day we will get there, wherever there is. Our ship will come in.

When I met my husband many moons ago, it was like coming home.

We instantly recognised each other. There he was. The magnetic pull was deafening. We had given each other another crack at it!

We, of course, were 'enlightened beings', and ready to work on the relationship.

Our kids, when we had them, would have none of our baggage, we would give them a pure start in life. So the books said.

Me, being such a high achiever, and he the same, would have an exemplary marriage. We would make it work. We would live a long life together, cleansed of our stuff, and it would all work out.

We travelled together, had children, ran a business together, did personal development courses together, chatted into the wee hours of the morning together, had lustful sex, and liked the same artwork. We are both curious beings and enjoyed challenging new concepts. Like marriage.

So why every now and then did we fight? Why couldn't he be happy like me, why couldn't he see the future together that I could?

Why did I feel happier OUT of the house than in it?

I loved him, to be sure. I felt his pain, to be sure. I willed him, with all the positivity I could muster to see the glorious future for us I held in my hands. If only he could believe that, all would be well.

We had counselling, we talked. We went around, and around, and around and around. We fought, we cried, we made love, we tried. We wanted to go forth. We wanted to be together. But it was like a glass wall lived between us. We could see each other, but not BE each other. I was lost for words.

I could not make it happen anymore.

I told him just how much I believed in him, loved him, but our dark place kept coming back. His relationship with our daughter got worse. Leaving seemed the best option. But when he tried, the tears would come.

**What do you do when you love someone, but you just can't MAKE IT WORK?**

High expectations, tools that don't work, and a revolving door of pain.

Pain we kept quiet to the outside world. You just don't let people know. You carry on.

There comes a time when you must let go.

There comes a time when you just, no matter what, have to let someone else go too. No matter what your desires, what your intentions, your dreams, your vision, you can lead a horse to water, but you can't make them drink.

**And what makes you think they want to drink at your waterhole anyway?**

I wondered what was wrong with me. Maybe if I was more attentive in bed, all would be well. Maybe if I took on more responsibility with the business and finances, all would be well. Maybe if I could just stop our daughter from aggravating him, all would be well. Maybe if the dogs stopped barking, more money came in, I got fitter, I cooked more, did the vacuuming more often, spent more time having 'fun', more time being close, it might just get better.

Maybe if I was more feminine, like other women, it might all work.

No. Still discussions around parting continued. No matter what I tried, I couldn't hold the threads together.

Exhausting.

**So I let go.**

I let go. Tenacious bugger that I am, I stopped trying to make it right for him.

And right for me.

I stopped pushing and pulling. And hoping.

Rolled over, surrendered and I let go.

I looked at myself. In the light of day, there was nothing more I could do.

I now had to BE with all of me, and stop hanging on.

I asked myself what I was willing to be in the relationship,

**I asked WHAT works for me,** and I let go.

So I sat down, and I wrote The List, just like I had written it all those moons ago, and listed all the qualities I looked for in a partner and asked whether I was willing to be all that myself.

> Sometimes it comes and rips you out of a warm bed, and throws you naked into a raging, freezing torrent. Without a life raft.

Then I asked:

**I'm curious, what needs to happen for someone like this to come into my life?**

**Someone whose values matched mine?**

**And I FINALLY let go.**

Some might say that was brave. Or idiotic. Or a relief. For me, that was the only choice left.

I was tired. He was tired.

So, jumping off the cliff and free falling is a precarious place to be, but to be open to change is to be open to everything. And change doesn't necessarily happen with kid gloves.

**Sometimes it comes and rips you out of a warm bed, and throws you naked into a raging, freezing torrent. Without a life raft.**

## Chapter Twenty Four:

# From the cosy, warm bed to the icy, raging torrent.

Leaving was never an option. I had left a marriage before, so not again.

So when he left me, the fog of Winter descended and I watched the life I had planned slip away like a log over a waterfall.

Gone.

I sat still for two days. Slowly systematically turning the Titanic around.

Emptying my life of togetherness and being still with me.

I rocked a lot.

*Entering The Void means giving it all up. And giving it all up means questioning everything, and I mean EVERY THING.*

**Entering The Void means giving it all up. And giving it all up means questioning everything, and I mean EVERY THING.**

Very, very quietly.

In the stillness of nothing arises the very stuff you just don't want to see.

I got to plumb my potency.

## Chapter Twenty Five:

## When in deep water, become a diver.

Thus began THE CHANGE.

Now, as I look back on that time, I marvel at our capacity to face it all. Some how we seem to function better when the truth is revealed. When all the cards are on the table.

He had met someone else. We were no longer two.

So I wanted to know it all.

I am not one to sweep things under the carpet. For now, I realise I wanted to milk this opportunity for all it was worth to bring up all the pain. All the resistance.

Everywhere I was playing it small. Everywhere I wanted control.

I questioned myself like a homicide detective. And my body, on high alert, sought the truth too.

I knew there was no hiding any more, for I was only hiding from myself.

Now I cannot and will not speak for my husband here. His is not my story to tell.

**But his courage to delve is what I discovered.**

He left for some time. Severed all ties and just sat. In a quiet retreat, with just paper and pens, and with the flood gates open, he wrote. And unravelled his life, his history, his hurts and his desires, and set himself free.

**A courage we women so often never see.**

**For we berate our men into being what we want them to be. Not who they really are.**

## Chapter Twenty Six:

# Who says nice girls can't get angry. Just watch me.

I was raised to be a nice girl. To accommodate, to share.

To take it on the chin. To turn the other cheek.

To smile and move on.

> *I never knew, but true anger is CLEAN. It comes up from the earth like a volcanic eruption.*

I never ever wanted to be called a Bitch.

I would rather die.

Now, how NICE is that? Recognise that one?

For brewing down below in the recesses of my body was a rage so potent, it could blow up the world. And if I went there, who knows what might happen?

Well, Providence has a big stick, to stir up the hornet's nest.

I needed something big, someone ruthlessly clever to wave the stick in my face.

**So, another woman appeared and decided my life could be hers.**

**Nice is not an option when THE GLOVES COME OFF.**

**I never knew, but true anger is CLEAN. It comes up from the earth like a volcanic eruption.**

It is like a dragon's breath of righteous desire that slays the fears that keep us small.

I pulled the plug and let my Bitch free.

And got to be the raging, gloriously expansive beast I truly be.

## I got to plumb my potency.

My family had been threatened, another woman had come into my life and said 'I'll have that'.

I got to see where that happened often in my life. I got to see where women are not nice, say things behind your back, and want what you have. I got to see where I was naive.

**I got to see where I hadn't been willing to own the Bitch in me either.**

**I got to see where I had been the victim of my own suffocating 'niceness'.**

> *I got to see where I had been the victim of my own suffocating 'niceness'.*

Someone else wanted what I thought was only my domain.

I got to face where I thought I was less than, passed over by a younger body, and no longer ENOUGH.

I got to see where I kept myself small.

Where I didn't demand of myself.

**Or declare my own VALUE.**

And I got to see where I too, many moons ago, had also been that woman. The other. I had to own her deception in me as well.

**The gloves came off. The Bitch stood still in all her glory and raged.**

**I raged at it all. But mostly I raged at me for playing it small.**

**And then time stood still.**

**And I watched myself.**

**I was cleansed at last.**

## Chapter Twenty Seven:

# When the jug is cracked, the water spills from it.

The poet Rumi once wrote that understanding is like water and our bodily existence like a jug. When the jug is cracked, the water spills from it.

So too, my marriage. My family.

The water flowed.

We ALL got thrown upside down.

Nothing was secret.
All was exposed.
Everyone had a voice.

All got to speak.

> *So what my husband and I did was simple. We returned to a place of choice. Where we could choose to be together, fully engaged, fully present in every moment. In every way. Nothing less. Transparent.*

It was all up for grabs. We ALL had to change.

**So what my husband and I did was simple. We returned to a place of choice. Where we could choose to be together, fully engaged, fully present in every moment. In every way. Nothing less. Transparent.**

**Or not.**

So we sat together for hours and energetically cleared everywhere we had done this to each other for lifetimes, or to others. We cleared the past. As much as we could find, with all the focus we could muster. Like terriers we scoured the landscape for anywhere we were stuck, anywhere we had held each other back.

The door had opened. We could blame each other, or we could challenge everywhere we remained small.

**A pivotal time.**

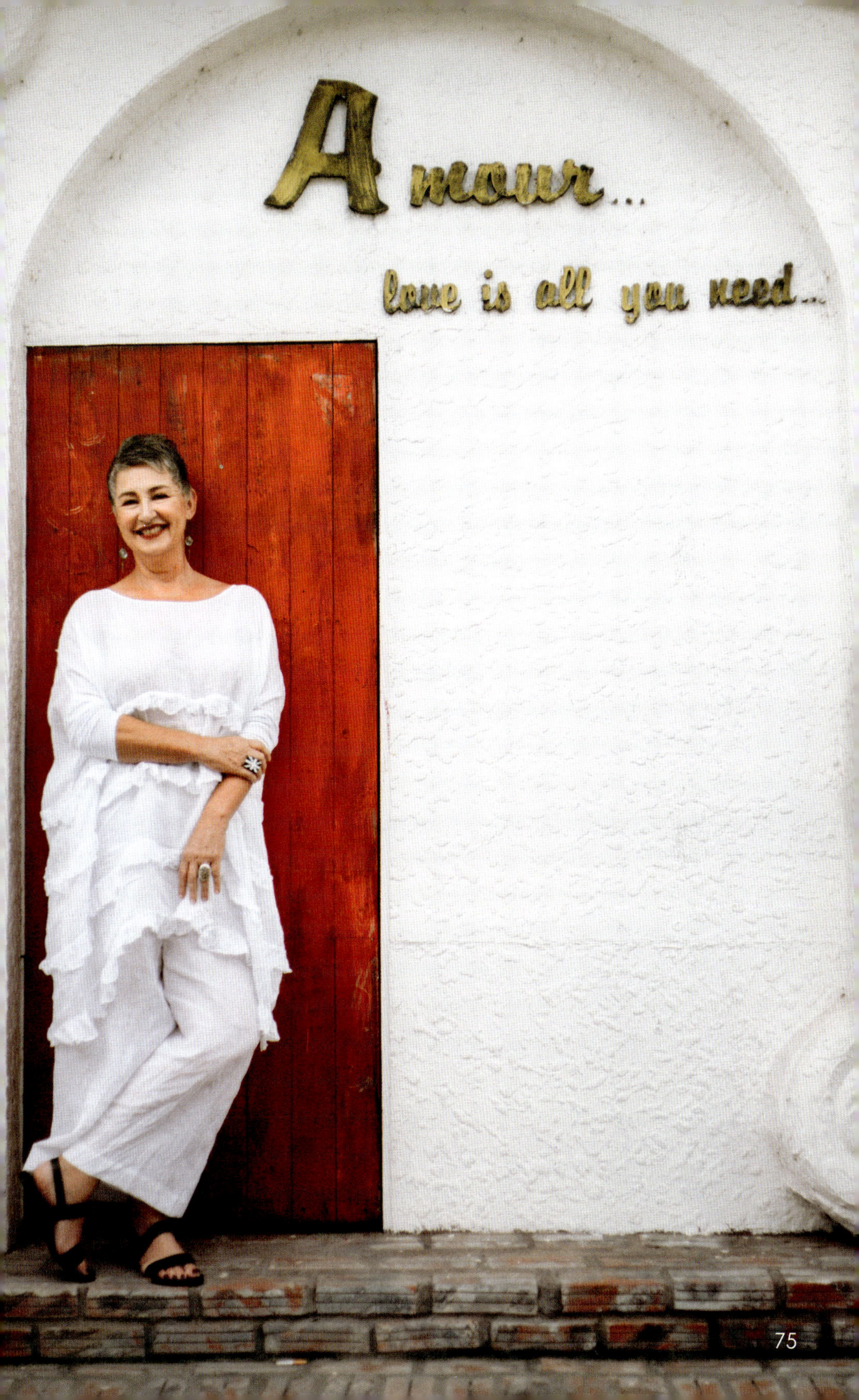
Amour...
love is all you need...

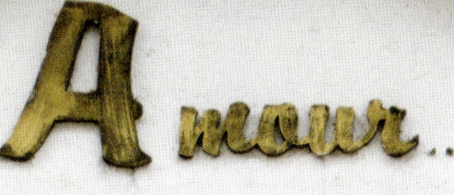

This was not only about us. This was about clearing stuff for everyone, everywhere. For generations.

No one was to blame. Nothing was taboo. All had to be revealed. The stuff we learnt about ourselves was liberating.

From a clear 360 degrees landscape, we got to say what really works for us.

Just us.

Not for society's norms, our kids' wishes, our family's name.
Nor our righteous desires.

None of that. We get to choose for just us. We don't really care what you think.

**And we now live each day, as just today. There is no past unless we make it so.**

I can remember the 'pain', and make myself feel less. Or not.

He can remember the 'guilt', and make himself small.
Or not.

> *You simply have to choose what works for you.*
>
> *And only you. And keep doing that. And let go of trying to control the outcome.*
>
> *Even if that means they might leave.*

In a true present, the past does not exist. There is only now.

So that is how we live our lives together, now. Every day a new day. A bit like that film Fifty First Dates.

That undeniable attraction we found for each other many moons ago is back. The intimacy can be extraordinary.

We are finally having fun. I am there to watch his back and he mine. I am there to help him with his dreams, and he mine. And what I learnt was this:

**You can't make someone want what you do.**

**You can't choose something for them when they are not given the space to choose for themselves.**

**You cannot hear the internal voices and the longing they do.
You simply have to choose what works for you.**

**And only you. And keep doing that.
And let go of trying to control the outcome.**

**Even if that means they might leave. They might meet someone else.**

**Or you must be the one to move on.**

**For on the big level, nothing can truly be lost, just wisdom gained.**

## I invite you to write something down.

Write down how you really want your relationship to be. And be prepared to be all of that yourself.

If you want kindness, write it down.

Great sex, humour, intelligence, courage, sensitivity, loyalty, someone who cooks, is creative, likes chocolate, travels, hunts fine things, is curious, cries in movies, loves shopping, children, art galleries, Italian Tenors, photography, smells, markets, whatever. Whatever it is, write it down.

**Please don't sell yourself short. Don't EVER see someone as more worthy than you.**

But be willing to be all of that too, whatever it takes. Then ask:

**What needs to happen for someone like this to come into my life?**

And get on with your life, being true to you. And watch what happens. It may not be what you expected, but it just might be better than you could ever imagine.

## Chapter Twenty Eight:

## Gratitude is not a fluffy word. It is a deep, sacred state of Being.

I once read a story about two little souls who loved each other dearly. It went something like this.

Both were in Heaven, and one said,

"I really want to learn about forgiveness."

The other said, "You can't do that here, you can only do that on Earth."

"But I want to, I need to!' pleaded the little soul, and her friend said,

"OK, tell you what, I'll come down to Earth with you and help you learn forgiveness. I will promise to do something so horrible to you, so awful, that you will have two choices, you can hate me for the rest of your life, or you can forgive me.

Forgiving me will be harder, but will set you free to be more of you. And forgiving yourself for not knowing better, will be the hardest, but it will set you free for all eternity.

The only problem we have, my dear friend, is that when we get to Earth, we will forget we had this conversation, **and we'll forget who we really are."**

**I choose now to see the bigger picture.**

I truly believe we are all here to help each other grow. We agree on some other level to do whatever it takes to wake each other up. And when we can be **GRATEFUL** for the messenger in **ALL** its forms, we are truly set free.

Grateful for the argumentative teenager, the nagging wife, the abusive boss, the unfaithful lover, the other woman, the pessimistic parent, the competitive girlfriend, the screaming child, the murderer, we are all here to push each other to choose something different.

And the energy of **GRATITUDE** itself sets all free. Transforms it all.

How else did Mandela walk free? Not through revenge and resentment, but through gratitude for himself and forgiveness for others. His key to freedom, his message for all.

I am now grateful for my husband. On a bigger soul level, he agreed to do the thing he knew would hurt me the most, at the time I needed it the most, so I would face my fears and grow. And from it flowed this book.

Now EVERY event, person, thought, reaction, fear on my behalf is welcomed.

I am grateful for them all.

> *Our stuff is just that. STUFF. You can look at it, and be grateful for it, and transform it.*

**Because they continue to show me the parts of me I refuse to accept. As hard as that is.**

Every part I have judged as wrong, every place I have hidden my fear. Everywhere I resist.

They are all just speed bumps in my landscape, a new game to play. **Embrace and welcome the speed bump and expand today!**

Oh, you may think I'm being flippant when I say that. Well believe me, I am not.

Our stuff is just that. **STUFF**. You can look at it, and be grateful for it, and transform it.

Or you can be ashamed of it. Hide it. Deny it exists.
Or blame everyone else.

Whatever. Your choice. No big deal.

But when you see it as just thought forms, energy, and behaviours you were simply unaware of, then it is the opportunity to grow.
To change.
You're going to have to face it sooner or later.

May as well be now.

And when you say you are grateful for it all. Use that word well.

For gratitude is not a word. Not a title of a fluffy pink book. Not a word to say so you can be nice.

**It is a deep State of Being. It is palpable.**

You know when you are truly grateful because tears will flow, and your heart will well up, and crack open.

For all the world to feel.

## Chapter Twenty Nine:

# Anger. So what if it was really your potency?

I had been taught to fear anger. To fear rage. To avoid conflict.

I was a nice girl after all. A private school upbringing in a middle-class family.

We didn't do rage in our house.

But how many times had that furnace simmered,
a slow boil, just below the surface?

And now it is out. All revealed. And there for all to see. Vesuvius erupted and cleared the path of lifetimes of debris just keeping me small.

*And now there's a place*
*I know I want to explore.*
*A place I'm not afraid of*
*any more.*
*A place of such intimacy*
*with me that all will be*
*reflected for me to see.*

For I am no longer afraid.

You can call me names, speak about me behind my back, leave me, betray me, try to silence me, or compete with me.

But you threaten my truth, and you will see in my eyes who I really am.

For I will no longer hide my light for anyone.

For I am bigger than the ocean, the planets, and the sun.

I am ONE with all. With everything and everyone.

To find that such rage and fury ignited a potency which set me free is a paradox just waiting to be shared.

THE GORGEOUS REVOLUTION

For this is a fierce deep love born of gentleness, vulnerability, knowing and truth. A force so strong it creates universes.

A place so deep and so glorious it sustains worlds across time.

So now there is nowhere to hide, nowhere to pretend.

I grew my wings. I now can fly.

**And now there's a place I know I want to explore. A place I'm not afraid of any more. A place of such intimacy with me that all will be reflected for me to see.**

## Chapter Thirty:

# The Potency of Singularity.

Sacred relationship is just that. Sacred.

And to have one, both must stand in the fire and not shrink back.

Sacred relationship within marriage is the fulcrum for spiritual growth in the express lane. Fasten your seatbelts. It's going to get rocky in here.

For all the escape routes just closed. No back doors, no hidden shutes, no sudden outs.

Commitment with a capital C.

And monogamy today is a very outdated term. The very sound of it is heavy.

It implies lack of choice.

For some, a death sentence.

Science says we are, after all, not wired to be with the same sexual partner for the rest of our lives.

So the term is now outdated, obsolete. Kaput.

I have come up with something else.

### The potency of singularity

Let me explain.

> *Sacred relationship within marriage is the fulcrum for spiritual growth in the express lane. Fasten your seatbelts. It's going to get rocky in here.*
>
> *For all the escape routes just closed. No back doors, no hidden shutes, no sudden outs.*

I enjoy sex. In fact, it is wonderful. It's a place that is deeply nourishing and intimate for me. It is liberating, deeply sensual, connecting, joyful and fun. Not always ground shattering, but for me, a place where I give, of myself to me, and of myself to another.
Before my husband, I explored a varied and healthy sex life. I have no hang-ups, no guilt. I enjoy sex.

Some say, what is the big deal? Sex is happening everywhere, all the time, in every moment. All over the globe.

An enjoyable pastime, fun between two people. I get that. Bodies like it.

For me, it is something else. I desire to help push the bounds of consciousness. To evolve a different way of being on the planet.

So what if I could have sex with someone, from a place of deep intimacy, and freedom, no baggage, no past or future?

Just now.

But what if I had been with that person for decades, so that our bodies knew each other, to a degree of vulnerability and gratitude that was palpable?

**What would be possible then?**

What might I learn about my body, what is possible beyond time, what is possible when two beings connect in the same exquisite space? What might be there? I ask.

For I don't yet know.

I don't know what is yet to come as I reveal more of me to someone who knows me already so well.

It's like going through the eye of a needle. Perhaps touching God. Perhaps being God.

Difficult, but possible. To go there, one must travel light. No guilt, no regrets, no shame. One must be willing to go where no one has gone before. What ecstasy can come from a level of intimacy between two, where no past exists?

**Yet where bodies have been together for lifetimes.**

I wonder.

A paradox surely to be posed if there was one.

So for me, this is what I choose. A level of intimacy, communion, and oneness so exquisite, I can only shut my eyes to imagine what it tastes like, feels like, sounds like, smells like.

And where will my body go, what secrets will it divulge, where will I travel? What strange energetic landscapes will we explore together, as one?

What can I gift? What can I receive?

When the walls truly come down.

I wonder.

So for me, I choose to be with just one person.
That is what works for me.

**I could be with many people, but just one will push the boundaries so much further.**

For that to be, I must let go even more.

And more.

I cannot choose for him. In fact, it would be fruitless to set boundaries for another. My husband is his own master. He now chooses what will work for him.

But the vulnerability I am willing to be is what I require in another.

The potency of singularity, to plumb the depths of what is possible with another who wants to go there too.

Let the walls come down.

**From a place of choice.**

And what man, given the invitation of bliss, the level of caring and comfort, the level of trust and vulnerability would not want that too? For it is the return to ourselves we are looking for, and it is the return to ourselves we will be.

**Evolutionary partnerships are changing the planet. In business and in the home. And sacred marriages will change the way we experience love. And possibility.**

**For nothing is forever. For forever does not exist.**

We do not own anyone. We cannot take them with us. We cannot promise a lifetime of commitment. Things change.

**But we can commit to be all we are right NOW.**

And more. And to watch each other's back. Be there when we falter, there when we doubt. Lean in, together, to the evolutionary edge.

**Lean in, hold each other tight, and set each other free.**

As Kahlil Gibran put it, "And let the winds of heaven dance between you."

I cannot hear the voice my husband hears when he quietly asks for him. Only he knows. His directions are his alone. And mine are mine. Yet when we ask from a place of truthful togetherness, the plan gets bigger. More doors open. More possibility exists.

> *Evolutionary partnerships are changing the planet. In business and in the home. And sacred marriages will change the way we experience love. And possibility.*

**It's that synergistic thing when 1 plus 1 equals 3.**

**A sacred trinity to behold beyond the bounds of time and space.**

When I said yesterday morning I had to leave that very day to write this book, he simply set about packing my food for me. No questions asked. He just supported me in what had to be done then and there. So as we surrender to a bigger story together, just maybe we will find something extraordinary. A life of unfolding joy, wonder, and gratitude to be shared. Because I know, that when we experience that much surrender together, the whole world will feel it.

It will open the doors for more and more kindness, vulnerability, expansion, and joy, for all.

**From a place of free will.**

**From a place of choice.**

Amen, sister.

## Chapter Thirty One:

# A few things my husband taught me about men.

Never, ever underestimate the sensitivity nor capability of men. Stop it right now. Stop buying his socks, his underwear, his shirts.

Stop ironing his clothes, and organising his razors. Buying his aftershave.

Stop picking up after him, making his bed, buying his mother's birthday present.

Stop organising his dreams.

**In short, stop mothering him. Stop it right now.**

You are cutting off his balls, and keeping him small.

You then turn to your girlfriends over coffee and whinge.

Whinge that he just can't organise himself out of a paper bag.

Why should he? You do it all for him. You are disabling him, and depriving yourself of a different possibility.

Take clothes shopping for instance. Now you may fancy yourself as a good shopper, and have a point or two about style. I thought I did. But my husband knew better.

And asked me to simply carry his bags. To not speak. Be invisible. To not offer a murmur.

To watch and observe.

So I did. And what I saw was endemic.

Please do not shop with your husband like he is six. Do not take clothes off the rack, and stack them all in the change room.

And liaise with the assistant, uttering help behind his back. I saw one woman stand behind her husband and pinch his pants in at his waist. Then cock her head to one side to see if she liked what she saw.

No. Please don't do that.

Just sit. And watch. Let him choose. And let him find the assistant. And let them flirt. Shut up and let him have fun.

Let him have the pleasure of buying his own clothes.

Oh yes, I hear all the time now that it is women who will change the world. That it is the feminine power the world now needs, of intuition, caring, allowing and creativity.

And what makes you think THAT is the domain of women alone?

To me, we are all equal. As an aware being, I am neither masculine nor feminine. I have ALL energies and choices available to me.

If a job requires action, doing and focus, I do it. It if requires allowing, creative collaboration and listening, I do it. Just because I am a woman, does not mean I cannot 'get work done'.

And just because my husband is a man, does not mean he cannot collaborate with a team, be creative, listen or be present with a small child.

Nor change a nappy, buy tampons, have women friends, vacuum, cook or clean up vomit. He simply does what is required. Without a point of view.

My husband is an intuitive man, a perfumer, and a body worker. He is also a gardener, likes science fiction movies, the odd cigar, red wine, a good game of football, a better game of poker, and a sock fight with our son.

He appreciates a back rub, a cup of tea, a good meal, a quiet word and a big hug.

### And to be left alone.

I have seldom bought him clothing, instructed him on what goes with what, nor questioned his parking capability. Unless invited. I rarely hang up his clothes. Nor iron them. I am careful not to navigate in the car when he is driving,

Unless he asks.

We learn.

Men are far more capable of many things than women give them credit for. We are arrogantly superior. We are critical and judging. We make jokes at their expense.

And we lament when they don't buy us flowers.

And we lament when they want comfort from someone else.

And we lament that they were not there for us.

But are we willing to be there for them?

In the still of the moment when they might need us most?

## Chapter Thirty Two:

# Receive. Receive. Receive.

This is not a chapter about bling.

This is, however, a chapter about a gift so much greater than all the priceless diamonds on the Earth.

**For understanding the true meaning of receiving will give you the world, the stars, the Universe itself.**

> *When you judge nothing, you can receive it all. Be aware of it all. Observe it all.*

Receiving is really about being aware. Of ALL energies. Of all possibilities.

Of your incredible potency.

Receiving requires lack of judgement.

**When you judge nothing, you can receive it all. Be aware of it all. Observe it all.**

Everything is available to you. You have full choice. You are not at the effect of anything. Nothing is right, and nothing is wrong. It all just IS.

**Receiving requires you to live in the present moment.**

It means to accept others as they are. To not try to change them. You cannot change anyone. They only change themselves.

And receiving you means to accept you the way you are too. Right now. **ALL of you.**

For when you truly receive you, you will open the doors to ALL of you, your bigger you.

The glorious YOU. The one who can receive all that is.

**And here is the rub.**

Women, most men simply want to adore you. They truly want you to be happy. Sometimes at their own expense.

Some will bend over backwards for you to hear their compliments. And this is the bit you must hear.

Men love your bodies.

Your curves, your wobbly bits, soft flesh, and warm buttocks. They love your freckles, your lines, your laughter, your touch. They love your smell. Your natural smell.

**They love you just the way you are.**

And if they don't, if they continually criticise you, or compare you to others in a demeaning way, **then leave them.** It is as simple as that. If they harm you in any way, please have the courage to leave. Seek help, and leave. I know that is difficult today, so please, please seek help.

When a woman accepts who she is, without judgement, when her body, no matter what the size, moves with ease, she will attract attention. From all men. And from all women. She will be noticed.

**And when she truly receives the attention and compliments from the man or woman she loves, her partner is happy.**

**They are acknowledged.**

**They are received.**

So, every time you complain about your body, or his, every time you are on a diet, wear ugly underwear, sad baggy tracksuits, cover your scent with synthetic toxins, or ignore his touch, you chip away a little at the very fabric of what was there, until you move apart, move away, and convince yourself he just doesn't understand you anymore. He's just not interested.

And he's not. He had his balls cut off ages ago, so he has forgotten how to be.

The TV looks a brighter option now.

For the partnership to be alive, it must be equal. Alive, engaged, moving, in question and curious.

For it to be deeply satisfying, it must be real. Honest, open, vulnerable, luscious, caring and present.

**And what if every time you made love, it felt like the first time?**

Because if there is just now, then it is. The first time. Always new, yet vaguely familiar!

*And what if every time you made love, it felt like the first time?*

**And what if everything you desired was at your fingertips, you just had to be willing to RECEIVE it?**

So before you complain about your partner again, make a list of all the things about him that you are grateful for.

**What's wonderful about him I'm not prepared to SEE?**

And focus on those. Then ask:

**What would need to happen for more of that to be present?**

And by giving him the space to choose for him, to get out of his way, and for you to get on with what makes YOU happy, something magical happens.

The man you have been looking for all along might just wake up beside you.

## Chapter Thirty Three:

# And a few things about family my children taught me.

> *When we are not real with ourselves, we are cheating those around us of a different possibility. We too must demonstrate what it means to be vulnerable, present, knowing, kind and brave.*
>
> *To dare to dream a bigger life.*

So what if you viewed them as their Big selves?

Not children, appendages, chips off the old block, money suckers or annoying distractions ... or L plate drivers.

**What if they knew way more than you, and your only job was to ensure every door was open to them?**

And what if you suspended ALL your points of view about them, and listened to them?

Really listen. What might you learn?

Who might you live with then?

When our son was eleven, he turned to my husband, and said, 'So when are you going to live your dreams, Dad"? My husband was gobsmacked.

They see us adults struggling with life, relationships, our bodies, our health, our money, with our dreams on the shelf.

And we take on the role of 'parents', know-it-alls, and be stern, exemplary, hovering, and firm. Telling them to go for their dreams, yet compromising ours.

It worked for a while, but not anymore.

**When we are not real with ourselves, we are cheating those around us of a different possibility. We too must demonstrate what it means to be vulnerable, present, knowing, kind and brave.**

**To dare to dream a bigger life.**

**Ours is now a 'kind house'.**

After the tumultuous changes, we declared our house a kind house.

The world may sometimes be nasty, competitive and mean, but **ours is a kind house.**

For if they cannot experience kindness here and now, in the sanctuary of their own home, what is the point?

How can they be that in the world if they do not experience that at home?

It wasn't always that way. And things took their toll.

Rampant tempers, frustrations, dreams not lived, posturing egos, and chains of time drew barriers between us, particularly my husband and our daughter.

Their relationship festered, going around and around. For what does a 51 year old man with no siblings, brought up by caring but isolated English parents, and no extended family know of a feisty 16 year old daughter?

Life does not prepare us for parenthood, and we flounder along the way. Beat ourselves up, and pray we'll do it better next time.

We want the best for our kids but bulldoze our way through, without asking a question.

We assume we know what is best for them.

We ARE parents after all.

**A breath of fresh air...**

So when life changed, when the barriers came down, a new quality appeared. A breath of fresh air.

One of respect, vulnerability, truth, renewed kindness, value, and above all gratitude for all.

**Ours is now a robust place of voice.**

No one is better than, more of an 'authority' than, smarter than, fiercer than.

No area is taboo. If one tries to be, they get reminded. Fast.

Conversations are rich, feisty, revealing and honest.
And sometimes painful.

But we have them.

And it takes time. The TV goes off, Instagram shuts down, and we talk.

We cook, we eat, we discuss, we laugh, we cry, we allow, we pay interest, we share dreams, we are honest.

We are there for each other. To help each other fill out our dreams.

And, please, it's NOT always rosy. We fall out of sync and have to remind ourselves of what really matters. We sometimes achingly go back to a place where all 'is not right'.

To recognise everywhere, we rub up against each other, cross each other, blame each other, is just another place to look where we ourselves resist.

Where we judge. Where we must be right.

Where our 'authority as parent' can trap us into not trusting a bigger picture.

Even brother and sister, can see past bathroom sharing limitations to a sense of caring. Jealousies are revealed, discussed and aired, and owned.

For at the age of three I'm sure she wanted to strangle her new brother. And if this was never acknowledged or resolved, the two would compete for life.

**So, what if they were just fellow timeless beings? Who might we all be then?**

Look into their eyes, and you will see something different.

**For every child, every teenager knows, somewhere beyond the cultural chains, what they are here to do. It is an indelible seed, a steadfast yearning that comes with their birth. And it is our job as parents to help uncover that seed.**

To invite them to live in wonder, to realise their dreams.

So we teach them to be different. To have the belief in themselves.

To be different in a world where sameness is safety.

To have the courage to swim against the tide.

Now with eyes wide open and consciousness to the fore, we seek out mentors for them, others who share our values, who can help them grow.

> *For every child, every teenager knows, somewhere beyond the cultural chains, what they are here to do. It is an indelible seed, a steadfast yearning that comes with their birth. And it is our job as parents to help uncover that seed.*

We seek out the village. For it is all not up to us.

We had days where they did not go to school. Days they simply had with us, or with themselves. To be quiet for a change.

We teach them about food. And manners, grace, cleaning up after yourself, toxic beliefs and who they really are.

We teach them to be grateful for all there is.

They teach us about computers, mobile phones, texting, resilience, generosity, and courage. Letting go, and 5.00 am risings to follow their dreams.

**And they learn that all of that teenage angst didn't belong to them.**

**To return it to sender.**

**For them to live in peace.**

To engage their desires, to have fun, to nurture their friendships, and to be resilient.

When all else fails, a hot cup of tea, a hug, a good laugh, a hot water bottle, an early night, a dog on your lap are all that are required.

Every day is a new day. A new possibility to get back on your horse, and get back on the track.

We teach them no one else will make you happy. Nor are they responsible for ours.

They are off the hook. They do not owe us anything. They are free to just be.

And within this moving framework of family, life goes on. Somehow, left to their own, rooms are cleaned, work gets done, meals are cooked, deadlines met, and we all move on.

Very soon, they will go. They will leave us alone.

They will head out the door and live lives of their own.

But what we have attempted to weave so far is a rich tapestry of respect, honesty, vulnerability and a genuine desire to see them be engaged in their lives.

To contribute to this planet as only they know how.

And one day around a big table yet to be found, I see us all, with partners, and grandchildren in raucous tow, raising our glasses to each other and life's rich possibilities. We will all acknowledge the courage in each other that is taken to live an honest, joyful, revealing life.

For our family now forges its own way in the world. We do not have to carry the torments, skeletons in closets, obligations, words not said, regrets buried, past hurts, disappointments, or dreams lost that the word 'family' so often has truly meant.

> *And if we choose to be together in the future, it will be done with free will.*

**And if we choose to be together in the future, it will be done with free will.**

A place of genuine desire to be with each other, with a generosity of spirit born of freedom of choice.

And a blueprint for our nation family, our world family, where all contribute to generating one kind human voice.

## Chapter Thirty Four:

# My Daughter and Me.

It's a pleasure to know her

This young woman I see

I see who she is

And she sees me

And that is the way

It will always be.

> *'Well, that is your experience. Please let me have mine'.*

I was driving my then ten year old daughter to school one morning, trying to explain the meaning of life to her. To head her off at the pass, so to speak. To save her some angst. Forget it. With calm determination she quietly said,

**'Well, that is your experience. Please let me have mine'.**

My daughter and I cannot, no matter how much we try, really dislike each other. We cannot sustain the lie. She is feisty and dramatic at home and behaves in an exemplary manner with others. An enigmatic, dyslexic, teenage grown-up.

And boy, is she aware. She can nail me in one. I cannot hide, I cannot run.

She sees through me every time.

And I, her. For our bodies know when we are lying.

So what is the point?

She has requested, just sometimes, that I be normal. So she has something to rebel against. So she can define and resist.
And pretend to struggle.

But she has learnt that it is just a waste of time.

For like one hand clapping, we allow her her choice. So she has to choose for her. She has asked quite clearly to let her experience be fresh. Hers alone. Not tainted by a parent's, 'I told you so'. Remember, she let me off the hook when she was just ten.

For she is gloriously wise. Tenaciously present. And awe inspiringly calm.

When she chooses.

Sometimes we have to sanitise her as she walks in the door.
The tendrils of school ground bitchiness hang off her like shards, piercing her brother will short, sharp mean girl daggers. But we remind her to ask,

'Who does that belong too?'

And the peace returns.

For the school ground and Facebook can infect lives with Chinese whisper poison, and teenage angst has nowhere else to go but enter homes.

She knows that's a choice.

So I celebrate her dreams. Her brightness. And she does not interfere with mine.

For hers is utterly an open book. And only she can write the words.

## Chapter Thirty Five:

## Teenage postscript. A request by our son.

When I was editing my book, our then fourteen year old son made a request. He asked me to tell you this story.

As mother and son, we have shared much. He nearly died at four when he fell out of a window, so my appreciation for fleeting life is probably magnified more than some.

So we love to play truant.

Not a huge believer in conventional education (you might have guessed), I sometimes called in sick for our kids and escaped for the day.

One week we went to the city. We explored food markets, Chinatown, drank coffee, and explored new precincts. We just wandered. We turned the music off in the car, and just talked. I gave him my time. He gave me his ear. He paid for my lunch.

And driving home, he said it was a day he would remember for the rest of his life.

**He asked me to tell you all this.**

Stop relentlessly organising your children's lives. Give them time just to be.

Take time off yourself, and show them your world. Show them the things that give you pleasure. Saunter. Reveal your dreams. Reminisce with them what they were like as a child, and help them remember the simplicity of warmth.

Every now and then, return them to the womb.

I remember one day years ago when he was just nine, it was exceptionally cold. A Friday.

All the mothers picked their kids up from school and were heading to the pool for swimming lessons. Because that is what you did. We all did. They were booked and paid for, and Fridays were about swimming. Full stop.

I remember my son came to the car and he looked at me. His swim bag was on the back seat. It was cold. Very cold.

Telepathy kicked in, we both smiled. We pulled out of the school gate and headed away from the pool. A lone car going the other way.

His smile got bigger. The hot chocolate we shared that day snuggled up in the cafe booth overflowed with marshmallows and warmed not only our bodies but our hearts as well. Swim classes can wait. Moments cannot.

*Stop relentlessly organising your children's lives. Give them time just to be.*

He wants me to tell you now, that the one thing kids want most in the world is to be heard, and you cannot hear them over the relentless drive of a parent's schedule.

And to be with them. Just them. No other sibling. Or smart phone, business deal or girlfriend. Just them. **To be present.**

So next time you are flying from soccer training to ballet to music concert to baseball to swimming class. Turn the other way. Go...escape. Be bad. Be naughty.

Break rules. And just for one day. One afternoon.

Be free.

## Chapter Thirty Six:

## It takes time to compete. Appointments all week.

Let's face it. Women compete. For attention, for attraction, for jobs, for sex.

And we learn it early, and we're masters at it. It starts in the home, kindergarten, grows at preschool, hits a fever pitch at fifteen, and leaves a lasting legacy for life.

We are so 'nice' to each other. We are so manipulatingly clever at masking our smallness but would cut each down in a heartbeat.

Behind backs, we are not 'nice' at all.

**Little girls compete with their mother for their father's attention.**

**They compete with their siblings for their mother's attention.**

**They compete with each other for their teacher's attention.**

**They then compete with other women for ALL attention.**

**They compete to feel better, to win favour, to prove value.**

**They compete to get men. They zealously compete to get men, to prove they are winners, yet again.**

And most men are oblivious. They are simply sitting ducks. They have no idea the lengths to which women will go to have them. And then discard them.

And this is at the heart of the matter. This is keeping us small.

And butchered. Who do women do cosmetic surgery for? Most women will say themselves.

They lie. They do it so they can feel good when comparing themselves to others.

Full stop.

If we did not compare, we would not need to compete.

**Everyone would be their own mountain peak.**

Women would stop asking, does my bum look good in this? They would revel in the pleasure of their bodies, and get on with what they are here to do.

Bodies would be hummingly happy, just the way they are, for no two are alike.

# Competing is a huge diversion from contributing.

**They live at opposite ends of the spectrum.**

**If I spend my time competing, my ego tells me where I am not. Where I lack. What needs fixing.**

**And the beauty industry tells you, everything does.**

**It ALL needs fixing.**

# For you will never be enough.

> *Competing is a huge diversion from contributing.*

Spend some time at a beauty counter with a white-coated 'professional', and you're surely going to feel great about yourself. After that is, you have parted with hundreds of dollars. You have actually paid to be quietly, subtly insulted by another woman. One in a white coat. With a superior sense of applying makeup. Precisely.

But you bought it. You bought the promise that you will look better, feel better, be younger, more desirable, have better sex, and have a happier life.

The industry has a name for it. It's called Hope in a Jar.

The truth is, the woman behind the counter has bought the story too. She is just doing what she is trained to do. She is trained to sell hope.

And then there are teenagers.
Teenage girls are brutal. Have you ever seen them prepare for the school formal?

It is ruthless.

The accuracy with which they know what to wear, how to apply makeup, is stunning. Apparently You Tube has some four million ways. And counting. Girls can text at the same time as applying mascara. And if they do not know, they feel less. Somehow Cinders won't be making it to the ball this year.....

This is the stuff of the young beauty industry. For they are in training. It keeps the industry alive and kicking.

If women didn't compete, sales of skin care and cosmetic surgery worldwide would plummet, economies fail. Hair straighteners would lie redundant on shelves, and fake tans would never see the light of day.

## Why then would I suggest we stop?

When we make all our choices from our **Bigger Me,**
all else falls away.

For we make it from a place of connection.

### A place of Oneness.

And we make our choices from an inclusive place. Not exclusive. And that includes our bodies' wellbeing as well.

I am not suggesting we give up beauty products.

My red lipstick brings me joy.

### What I am suggesting is that we give up competing.

Comparing, judging, rewarding external beauty and being driven to fill our bathroom with every conceivable toxic substance known to chemists.

To fit in. To be safe. To be loved.

For when we stop comparing, we stop playing small.

**We are our own mountain peak.**

And we can get on with the job we are here to do. That requires co-creation, collaboration, working as a team. It requires listening open-heartedly to others, to our daughters, our mothers, our girlfriends, partners, ourselves.

It involves listening to our heart's desire and putting THAT first.

And if you think your heart's desire is to look better than everybody else, then **LISTEN AGAIN.**

**Indeed if women are going to change the world, we had better get over ourselves.**

## For it takes time to compete. Appointments all week.

Manicure, hair, facial, massage, waxing, the gym. Pilates, yoga, zumba and boxing. And meditation for the conspicuously spiritual component. My 'special me' time.

Add in kids, the soccer run, girlfriends, job, home, fast food takeaways, internet, emails, cable TV and pet walking, and **we don't have much time left.** Even for partners. Let alone us. Let alone for the planet.

No wonder the world is in the state it is.

So what do I suggest you do?

Here goes. This is what I know.

> *Indeed if women are going to change the world, we had better get over ourselves.*
>
> *For it takes time to compete. Appointments all week.*

## Chapter Thirty Seven:

# Let's start Our Revolution. Right now.

### 1. Stop weighing yourself.

Just stop it. Throw the scales away.

You won't die, you won't explode, you won't ravage the nearest biscuit barrel, the tub of ice cream, the deli of salami.

In fact, your body will show up happier than ever if you just involve it in every part of your life. So stop measuring it, and start talking to it.

> NO food is good or bad.
> All food is available to you.
> Including chocolate.

### 2. Ask your body.

You are going to ask your body what it wants to eat. It knows what it requires.

### 3. Get out of its way and ask it a question.

And listen.

Feet together, eyes closed, ask it a yes/no question...

Body, will it be nourishing for you want to eat this food?

It will lean forward for yes, and backward for no. Or it will give you a picture.

What if all food tasted deliciously orgasmic? What if every mouthful was a joyful experience? I'm not joking.

### 4. Then BE PRESENT. Sit down when you eat. And eat slowly. Quietly.

Then stop when it starts to taste like chewy cardboard. It may be after only three mouthfuls. Your body has had enough. Just put your spoon down and stop. The children in Africa won't

be saved any more if you just stop.
Our bodies require way less than we think. Especially when we are present in our lives and stress-free. We just eat less.

**NO food is good or bad. All food is available to you. Including chocolate.**

If you ask your body, it will guide you to the foods it needs to be well. The foods that have the vitamins, the minerals, and the energy it requires.

**5. Your body is now your friend, your constant intelligent guide.**

Treat it with respect. Value it. Honour it. Nourish it. Delight in its new connections.

**6. You are not your past. Let it go now.**

> *You are NOT your story, your past pains, your need to be right. You are now none of that. Drop the cloak and walk free. Just like that.*

**You are NOT your story, your past pains, your need to be right. You are now none of that. Drop the cloak and walk free. Just like that.**

You have no past demons to assuage, no pains to heal, nor dark holes to fill.

You are complete as you are. Truth be, there is nothing wrong with you.

There never was.

**7. Rediscover the pleasure of food.**

Sometimes I eat peanut butter, gooey, runny French cheese, smooth dark chocolate. Mostly it is rice, meat, fish, chicken, grains, fresh vegetables, greens, avocado, fruit, tahini, eggs, homemade soups, legumes, rice crackers, and yoghurt. Good full milk yoghurt. And water. And sometimes red wine.

Just ask your body what it wants.

## Chapter Thirty Eight:

## Food is Great.

I eat butter and full cream milk. I eat food as close to its natural state as possible. We rarely eat out.

We all cook in our house. Food is great. It is creative, luscious, vibrant, and restores my soul.

We watch cooking programmes together and marvel at overseas culinary delights.

We search out different ingredients. We taste different tastes.

I enjoy a glass of red wine when I feel like it. It too restores my soul.

One of the best movies I have seen was 'It's Complicated', with Meryl Streep. Please watch it. She is one extraordinary woman.
If she reads this book, she would smile that beautiful, whimsical smile of hers.

Because she knows what I am talking about. I nod my head to you, Ms Streep.

She made chocolate croissants from scratch with such lust, such enjoyment, such sensuousness, I could barely contain myself.

I used to bake our own bread when the kids were young. It was one of the most sensual things I have ever done. I would knead it and caress it, and let it rise to a baby's bottom. I loved it.

Its smell would permeate the whole house with warmth. I remember when our son was two, he would wait for the bread to come out of the oven, and I would slice it open. Steam coming from its soft inside, he would climb up on the bench and nestle his nose in its wheaty warmth and sigh. We would look at each other with bliss, cut off the crust and share it with butter, lots of butter. And Vegemite.

And we ate slowly. Savouring every mouthful.

Now we all cook. We love food. Both our children, when little, have eaten whatever we have. We have never had a kids menu.
They ate oysters at four, and fresh sardines, pipis, pate, and kidneys. They eat vegetables, goat's cheese, chilli, and sashimi. They just love food. And both have wonderful bodies, guilt free. They have learnt to ask their bodies.

And when they don't, they pay the price of feeling unwell.
Their choice.

I digress just a little. I want to thank my mother for introducing me to food. And my grandmother.

My mother couldn't cook when she first got married in the fifties. So she learnt. She took French cooking lessons. And like Julia Childs, she fell in love with cooking. My father adored it. It was what kept him going.

He was, from his mid-twenties, dying of cancer. In those days, one just accepted inevitable death. I'm sure her food kept that smile on his face.

My English grandmother too was a great cook. Her Yorkshire puddings were the stuff of legends.

So my mother made chocolate mousse, coq au vin, chicken marengo, and quiches to live for. Her pastries were exquisite. Her béarnaise sauce was extraordinary. We ate oysters, camembert, olives and black pudding.

She was always, always surrounded by cookbooks. She was quite simply in her element. And even though later, as I relentlessly dieted, I still was influenced by her love of food, and the deftness with which she knocked up a sponge, a pavlova, a simple rice salad. She was a culinary genius.

For all the years of dieting, of denial, of guilt and control, lead me away from my culinary soul. Food is an expression of God. Nature's cornucopia. Choose it well.

# THE GORGEOUS REVOLUTION

**Our Gorgeous Revolution will see us return to the kitchen. The garden, the soil, the hearth. The earth. For simple fare, born of pleasure and sharing.**

When our kids were little, my husband had a biodynamic garden. He was at home there. He grew all manner of wonderful things. He would be gone all day in the garden, and bring home produce in a big, big bucket.

We would have potatoes fresh from the soil, zucchini just picked, and occasionally more than we bargained for. The odd tiny green frog would hop from our plates, having rested in a lettuce leaf for the journey home.

> *Our Gorgeous Revolution will see us return to the kitchen. The garden, the soil, the hearth. The earth. For simple fare, born of pleasure and sharing.*

I applaud Jamie Oliver and his Food Revolution. It makes me cry to see our kids cannot cook, cannot recognise a vegetable.

The whole world needs to get behind such grass root movements and get us back in the garden, back in the kitchen, and back at the table together.

We have to take back the sourcing of our food. The growing of local produce. We have to stop buying pre-packaged chemical concoctions and eat from the earth. Fresh. We need to get our fingers dirty again and our feet in the soil.

And even grow hydroponic tomatoes on our balconies.

Food is Energy. Life force. Medicine. Let us surround ourselves with fresh produce.

Let us all learn to grow.

When eaten with curiosity and an open mind, food introduces us to new concepts, new smells, tastes, cultures, new sensations. It is extraordinary stuff. All provided by the universe to help us expand, to be sustained and to live an exuberant, vital life.

I just don't get that from a packet, a fast food store, a long life shelf.
A diet drink.

Don't short change yourself any more.

Stop dieting. Educate yourself about food. Try new things.

Learn to cook.

And above all, **ask your body.**

**And it will dance with a lightness not born of this world.**

## Chapter Thirty Nine:

# Our Revolution Continues. Have More Sex. Full stop.

I'm going to pose something different here. A truth we have veiled for way too long.

Sex is not dirty. It is not sinful, vile, revolting, nor taboo.

**Just WHO does that belong to I ask?**

> *We are all energy. We exchange it all day long, whether we are aware of it or not.*
>
> *Nature is reproducing itself all the time. It is having sex all day long.*

Sex is happening everywhere, all round us. All the time. It is age old. It is universal.

It is a part of life. Without it, life itself does not happen. It is generative, explosive, gentle, nourishing. And joyful.

**Remember, sex is really about RECEIVING. Receiving you.**

Let me explain.

**We are all energy. We exchange it all day long, whether we are aware of it or not. Nature is reproducing itself all the time. It is having sex all day long.**

Plants, insects, animals, birds, bees, amoebas, all life forms are generative.

And that includes us.

But somehow, we have lost our way.

In our world, 'sex' has become a commodity, a desired outcome, a thrusting, lusty act which has turned us off. Or on.

Yet not in a kind way.

We buy it, sell it, want it, compete for it, can't get enough of it, have none of it, lust after it, and refuse it.

At best we have it 2.6 times a week, at worst, we hung up our vaginas years ago.

Well, I'm here to tell you, you need more sex.

Let's however, make a distinction here. Because I do. A big distinction.

**Again...Sex is about RECEIVING. About receiving energy.**

**Intercourse is about putting your genitals together. And they are not necessarily the same.**

I have said several times we are energy. And to be connected, to be aware, to be listening, the more we are aware of that energy, those vibrations, the more we will expand consciousness on the planet.

It is that simple.

Your body receives energy. When you stop receiving, you will eventually die.

So, stay with me here. There is a very big distinction about sex that can set you free.

It set me free when I heard it. It explained everything about sex I felt I had been missing.

## Chapter Forty:

## Sexuality and Sensuality. The difference will set you free.

They are two sides of the same coin, but entirely different energies.

**Sexuality is about COMPETITION.**

From a woman's point of view, Sexuality is strutting your stuff. It is about the boobs, the vagina, the lips.

Sexuality requires pushing.

Attraction as well, but mainly pushing. It is overt. It is calculated. It is manipulative. Its primary goal is to get attention, to get what you want. It is usually about acquisition, control, and sometimes physical sex.

Sexuality implies power over.

And this is where men can be sitting ducks. They are unaware of some women's real intentions. Their thoughts go south, their minds turn to sex, and they follow their noses home to the pot at the end of the rainbow. The Golden Vagina. She has him by the short and curlies again. Only this time it is his penis in the trap.

And maybe his future.

He is a trophy, an acquisition, a relationship in the wind. Sexuality is a game. You can play it or not. Just make sure you are not at the effect of it. Because the very nature of it implies someone has power over someone else.

And its cousin is porn. Rampant, often brutal porn. Where men have power over women, but really have relinquished themselves to a manufactured ideal of what intimacy is. Brutal mechanical acts of automation.

# THE GORGEOUS REVOLUTION

We are confused, disconnected, driven by media and starved. Starved of nourishment or feather touch. And starved of just being at home with ourselves. Present.

**However, Sensuality is about receiving and reciprocal flow.**

It is open and vulnerable.

It invites, insinuates, and is gentle, kind, nourishing, nurturing, joyful, playful, healing and fun. And orgasmic, generative and expansive.

Sensuality does not necessarily include having sex. It is a choice.

Sensuality can be felt in the caress of a fabric, the lilt of a song, the perfume of a flower, in the creamy foam of a coffee.

*However, Sensuality is about receiving and reciprocal flow.*

In your ability to be present with you. To receive you. To receive energy.

To connect.

Sensuality is available to all, all the time, 24/7.

Oh, let me count the ways. It is about warmth, the sun on your back, the languid stretch of the cat, the perfection of the imperfect. Acceptance of what is.

It is a smile, an open, spontaneous smile. Sensuality allows for no judgement of her body. She is present, **without judgement,** in the moment. Her body hums.

It is receptive. **Vulnerable.**

She may be large breasted, flat chested, big, little, gay, blonde or bald. It has nothing to do with her exterior beauty.

In fact, some technically beautiful women display no sensuality at all.

It has all to do with her connection to life. Expansive life. Sensuality is the way she moves her body, lifts her head, talks to children, touches her neck, smooths her skirt, pats the dog, makes love to a cake, or strokes your arm. It is the way she wears her clothes, her hair, tilts her ankle, or folds the washing.

And the way she is present with you.

Women who breathe sensuality are aware of their attraction. But care not for results.

**They just be.**

So, it is the motion you see when one is one with the universe.

In the words of the glorious Jean Houston, 'evocative ebullience' just flows from their loins.

When a woman makes love from a place of reciprocal sensuality, it is like coming home to roost. A surrender. A connection with the very life force itself, an orgasm of universal magnitude.

So why, oh why do we deprive ourselves of that?

We don't have to.

**Sensuality is everywhere. Available to everyone. Men and women.**

**Just not necessarily in the magazines. Sensuality doesn't get airbrushed.**

So, here we go.

More sex, that is, more receiving in your life doesn't necessarily require a partner. But if you have one available, they will thank you.

Firstly, you are going to get to know your body. Without judgement, without shame.

> *You ARE love itself.*
> *End of story.*
> *How can you NOT love you,*
> *if you ARE IT?*
>
> *That would have to be the Number One Cosmic Joke of the largest enormity.*

I remember years ago when I was first starting out on the personal development 'journey', someone said...'You have to love yourself, love your body'.

Sure, try telling that to a serial dieter with bulimic tendencies. Well, I'm going to make this real easy. A short cut so to speak.

**You ARE love itself. End of story. How can you NOT love you, if you ARE IT?**

**That would have to be the Number One Cosmic Joke of the largest enormity.**

**It took me years to get that. Please save yourself the time and the effort.**

**You are one with God, one with the Universe, one with Love, and one will ALL.**

**Your religion may not agree with me, but last time I looked, there was still a vested interest in keeping you small.**

So now we have that straight, to love yourself is a no brainer.

To accept your body comes next.

So talk to it. Remember what we said, it is your best friend.

Find out how it works.

Examine it. Every inch of it. In a mirror. Caress it, touch it, stroke it, with care, kindness, and wonder.

Take your time. Feel its energy. Its lightness. Its language. Its hum. And just be with it quietly.

Be still.

Now thank it. Let it reveal its secrets. Let it cry tears of joy.

Tears of relief.

Now promise to give it pleasure for every remaining day you are together on this earth.

**Real pleasure, gentle pleasure, palpable pleasure.**

Let it move, sway, dance, rock. Let it smell the roses, the coffee, the earth. Let it feel silk between its fingers, cashmere between its thighs, and place jewels and pearls upon its skin.

Or at the very least, gift it gratitude.

Just say thank you.

## Chapter Forty One:

# The Little Black Dress and God

God made everything, including the Little Black Dress.

Do not wait for a special occasion to wear yours. If your body desires one. Wear it around the house. Alone. Or not.

And remember, one pair of exquisite shoes that make you move with ease and grace are worth more than 100 that don't.

> *Dispense with clutter.*
> *Keep only the clothes that resonate with this new found sensuality.*
> *This new found nourishment.*

One beautiful French dress that you can wear again with sandals or high heels is a greater investment than all the executive stuff your image consultant said you should wear.

One handmade hat, with a sensual lilt beyond compare, is all your sweet head will ever require.

Just make it a beautiful one.

**Dispense with clutter. Keep only the clothes that resonate with this new found sensuality. This new found nourishment.**

Get rid of things that you are hanging onto, like jeans you never wear, clothes you never fit. Corporate straightjackets that hide your curves, and make you comply.

Moisturisers half empty on your shelf.

**Take your body shopping for a change. Not, by the way, with your 'girlfriends'. They may be challenged by this new you, threatened by your shift, feel lessened by your courage.**

**No, just go alone.**

But find yourself a brilliant shop assistant. One who will tell you The Truth. One who caresses the clothes in her care, and welcomes the new you into her shop.

Who smiles at you, genuinely. Because she is there to help you transform.

Invest in the best supportive, beautiful underwear you can buy. Wear it, and wash it with love.

> *Take your body shopping for a change. Not, by the way, with your 'girlfriends'. They may be challenged by this new you, threatened by your shift, feel lessened by your courage.*
>
> *No, just go alone.*

Familiarise yourself with fabric. Cashmere, velvet, silk, organza, pure linen, French cotton, pure wool. And soft, pliable buttery leather. Second hand will do. Many of my favourites are treasured finds from the recycled store. They have history in their folds, grace in their linings. Beauty in their buttons.

**Buy natural fibres. Feel the difference against your skin.**

Wonderful clothes do not have to cost a fortune. I once helped a good friend clean out her wardrobe. I left with the most beautiful purple velvet shoes you have ever seen, and a black cashmere coat, and a ten year old Prada bag that needed a new home.
They are three of the most pleasurable items in my wardrobe.

For that I am grateful.

**Make dressing simple. Simplify your wardrobe. Arrange the clothes in colours. Buy good hangers and let them all face the same way. No, I am not anally retentive here. Just restore order and calmness to your wardrobe, so dressing becomes a pleasure.**

**Talk to them. Your clothes. Your friends.**

**Above all, wear them.**

I do not have many clothes. But what I do have, I love.

I wear black often. I feel good in it. It is easy, delicious, and for me, very sensual. When I wear colour, it is with a purpose. My body will choose it.

Every day I ask my body what it wants to wear. I take it off the rack, put it on and go. Some of my clothes are ten years old.

I do not collect shoes. I only have two feet. Should I find myself with too many, I simply pass them onto someone else. They let me know when they are ready to go.

I will pay $500 for a dress, or $50, or $5. I don't have a point of view. My body wears the clothes, not the other way around.

I only buy what my body really wants. Not me.

I went to Paris and London a few years ago. For the very first time. I love clothes. You may have gathered that they are a joy to me. But the older I get, the more refined my taste, the less I see that I truly desire. Just like food, when you allow yourself ANY choice at all, then you can have it all, or none.

A little or some.

The only clothes I remember in the whole of London and Paris was a light angora vest, a soft fur so cloud like, it was like breath against my skin. And Armani brogues in midnight blue. Now they too were nice. Very nice.

I didn't buy any clothes in Paris, but a pair of woollen socks. The best most glorious socks I have ever owned. They were all that my body required.

**But I took the energy of it all with me. For the rest of my life.**

Ah, but I digress. By now you have the picture.

Sensuality can be lying in a warm bath, basking in the golden glow of a beeswax candle, or lying naked in the sun. It can be giving a wonderful, heart open speech from a place of authenticity that fills the room with desire to do good. To be more.

**To contribute.**

It is to be vibrant, open, nourishing, real, intelligent, and aware.

Be aware of simple pleasures and rituals and pursue them.

Like good sheets. Soft, crisp sheets.

**Dressing a bed is like dressing a body. Have the most beautiful linen you can find, and change it at whim. Nest well.**

**Life has a rhythm you can find when you pare away the crud, simplify the rules, and focus on The Truth.**

**Choose what nourishes you, feeds you, nurtures you and is kind.**

Choose what heals you.
Lifts your spirit.

And seek nothing less.

**So when it comes to having sex, please don't short change yourself.**

**Ask for someone who is compatible with you.**

> *Dressing a bed is like dressing a body.*
> *Have the most beautiful linen you can find, and change it at whim.*
> *Nest well.*

Allow yourself to receive. Allow yourself to be caressed, nourished, languidly licked, deliciously stroked. To explore. To laugh. To nuzzle.

To be held.

To spoon.

To have FUN.

And be willing to give all of that too.

**And make the time. If your life is too busy for languid sex, change it. Quality, not quantity. Pleasure, not chore.**

**Sex is about receiving you.**

**And when you receive you fully, you will experience joy.**

**That is all there is to it.**

And your children will sense there is a new energy in the house, and they will feel safe. They too will be nourished by your sensualness, your warmth, and your care.

They too know and feel when the house is happy.

> *And make the time. If your life is too busy for languid sex, change it.*
>
> *Quality, not quantity. Pleasure, not chore.*
>
> *Sex is about receiving you.*
>
> *And when you receive you fully, you will experience joy.*
>
> *That is all there is to it.*

And your partner? They will hopefully be ready. They may take some coaxing, some guidance, some exploration. You need to teach them to receive as well.

To also be with their body in present time.

**To receive a gentle, kind, caring touch.**

Because that is what our partners need too. To be shown the art of gentleness. Sensual slowness, and breath.

To be with their bodies, to be one with you too.

To be vulnerable.

It will take time. Make time.

Feathers help. Or simply find a partner who already knows. Maybe they have been there all along, just waiting for you to slow down.

To stop pushing, preening, poking, smoothing, criticising.

**For you to receive them.**

## Chapter Forty Two:

## Menopause. Bring it On.

I am not a medical doctor, a naturopath, or health expert of any kind.

I am simply a woman who has learnt to listen to, nurture and honour her body.

I can tell you what I know from my own experience. It may resonate with you, or not.

> *I am however becoming more aware that the more I engage my heart's desire, speak my truth, am curious and ebullient about life, I transform.*
>
> *Not from a pill, not from botox, nor lasering, nor fillers, but from the strength of my own light.*

I have not menstruated since I was 52 years.

When I had my first flush, I went to my homeopath and took sepia. I have not had a hot flush since.

I had my son at home in a tub at 40, and my daughter at 36 in a birth centre, with hypnotherapy.

In my sixth decade, I enjoy richer sex than I have ever known, and look forward to even more.

I eat well, rest, take baths, have mentors, good friends, anoint my body, and live by the sea.

**I do not concern myself with aging, I simply recognise each stage as it appears.**

**I am however becoming more aware that the more I engage my heart's desire, speak my truth, am curious and ebullient about life, I transform.**

**Not from a pill, not from botox, nor lasering, nor fillers, but from the strength of my own light.**

**My own connection to generative life itself.**

**Radiance you CANNOT buy in a jar!**

But what I have had is time, and a deep desire, to get to know my body. And me.

The bigger me.

I have released past hurts, energetic blocks, niggly pains, and past regrets.

**I do not judge myself. Anymore.**

**I am enough.**

And I have followed my dreams. I have followed my path, relentlessly. I have followed that inner voice for as long as I have known and I have taken action accordingly. And often against
the familial grain.

**I have learnt I will never have my mother's absolute approval, nor her understanding. Nor her warm acceptance. For now.**

I have learnt no one will ever truly see what I see, nor hear what I hear.

I have learnt to acknowledge all other women's jealousies of me or each other, as just a place they refuse to be all they too can be.

It is just a choice.

And whatever daggers they throw at me, pass through me. They no longer stick.

And I have learnt to welcome the words of some wise men and women into my life with regularity. I choose my inner sanctum carefully.

I have a fire in my belly, and it has somewhere to go.

I belong to no one. And no one to me.

I have a plan. A voice. I am engaged with life itself.

**I no longer have to be nice. I am willing to be fierce. Very fierce if required.**

I am willing to live a larger life. To do whatever is necessary to expand life for me.

Joyfully.

I choose to be all of me and more. Much more.

**I no longer play small, so others will not feel less. That is not my problem anymore.**

> *I no longer have to be nice.*
> *I am willing to be fierce.*
> *Very fierce if required.*
>
> *I no longer play small,*
> *so others will not feel less.*
> *That is not my problem*
> *anymore.*

I will not apologise for my talents, my intellect, my body. I will use them, expand them and continue to be an instrument for change in a world where I can truly be a difference. A difference that only I can be.

**Because I have learnt that it's not about me.**

**All that I am is not about me.**

**Remember. I am simply an instrument to bring Heaven to Earth.**

**A simple tool to bring about change.**

# So before you say, well, that's all OK for you, but what about me? STOP.

Just where did you go?

If I can do it, so can you.

**But only YOU can choose.**

Not me.

**But TOGETHER, we can be a mighty team.**

**So, move it, yes, YOUR body. Move it. Get ENGAGED.**

**Ask for what gets you going and GO.**

Get the fire ignited in your belly, transform those pent up hot flushes into energy and fuel, and follow that dream relentlessly. Draw those boundaries in the sand, and dig deep.

Ask questions. Seek engaged knowledge. Read. Explore alternatives.

Plumb your depths.

Let go of your angst. Let go of control.

Follow the truth. Ask your body what IT wants.

Now.

**What are you waiting for?**

## Chapter Forty Three:

# The Beauty Cocktail. Are you drunk enough yet?

George Orwell once said

> " **In a time of universal deceit, truth telling becomes a revolutionary act.** "

What I am about to tell you will set you free.

Get you off the Beauty Grid.

You will never have to buy a dodgy jar of cream again.

You will now be able to see your way through the perfume maze, keep your head above the anti-aging claims, and never have to subject yourself to 'ever so constructive' all pervasive beauty ridicule again.

*"In a time of universal deceit, truth telling becomes a revolutionary act."*

But be warned, what I say may not please you, might challenge you, and will rock your perfumed world. If you don't want to know, then don't read on.

**No one in the beauty world speaks to me. No one.**

I am invisible, off their radar, not featured in their demographic, nor invited to their openings.

But somewhere I get the strange feeling I am not alone.

I get the feeling that out there is a group of women silently frequenting the department stores too.

Searching for a skin care brand that is compatible with them.

One that doesn't shadow the truth, make grandiose claims, nor talk condescendingly down to them. One that charges you for fine ingredients, not marketing, and glossy magazine covers. One that works with Nature and not against it.

And, very importantly, one that is sexy, has no false bottom, is luscious, and voluptuous, and ambrosial, and truthful and generous, and one that doesn't claim a thing.

**And one that makes your body sing.**

And that works. That moisturises your skin.

Ah, but I digress yet again...

I should know the beauty world well. I used to work in advertising for a skin care and perfume giant, and have been an avid user of product since I was 13.

The amount of beauty and fashion magazines I have devoured could wallpaper my entire house. And the garage.

Years ago, I was on the other side of the discreet one way mirror in those comforting focus groups. The ones the nice person asked you to talk about your skin, over wine and crackers. You talked about your skin care worries, your underbelly.

Your deepest aging fears.

I have seen it all.

Yet no one speaks to me now.

**For I am off the Beauty Grid.**

*I cannot be persuaded, cajoled, threatened, cautioned, favoured, pushed nor pulled into believing that I am less. For that is what the beauty world does. It plants a little seed of doubt and builds it until you are hooked. You are in. Because you are special, you are worth it.*

**I cannot be persuaded, cajoled, threatened, cautioned, favoured, pushed nor pulled into believing that I am less. For that is what the beauty world does. It plants a little seed of doubt and builds it until you are hooked. You are in. Because you are special, you are worth it.**

You are worth the expense, the time, the new colours, the research, the seduction, the white coats, the expensive packaging, the patent pending claims, the marketing dollar, the hype. For without you, there wouldn't be an industry. So we covet you, oh wrinkly goddess. With our loving care for you, all will be well.

My husband makes my skin care. From roses.

No one really knows much about us. But we have been compared to the two largest brands in the world on blogs and came out, well, surprisingly well.

You see when we launched our brand many years ago, I told everyone. The beauty editors, the magazines, the newspapers, the department store owners, the fashion designers, the airline in store suppliers, the biggest and most glamorous spas in Australia, and all stockists, without exception, said no.

**You see, I told the Truth.**

I told our story, I told the Truth.

And being small, expensive, Australian and not French was a parochial error we could not singlehandedly fight, without hundreds of thousands of dollars at our disposal. The retail doors shut tight. The beauty backs turned on a brand not worthy of mention in the bigger story of spin.

For the first casualty in the beauty world is the one of Truth.

So we stayed small. Under the radar. And waited.

Waited for the right time to voice our story again.

**Now…don't fib…I know you don't read labels.**

For if you did, you would know that most creams are 90% water, or should I say aqua. Even the expensive ones.

I'm not a real whizz at figures, but I can measure a 50ml cream, even one with a false bottom.

And see that the price I am paying might just be a bit hefty for that much water.

What you are really paying for is marketing. The advertising dollar, the industry deals, the sales promotions, the need to be heard above the cacophony of latest mind blowing claims.

Having worked in advertising, I have a fair idea of what a glossy full page ad costs these days.

Now if you're Ok with that, let's continue.

Most creams, by the way, have to have a shelf life of around three years. They have to be stable to travel and satisfy aesthetic norms. In other words, they must look clinically pretty, and seductively professional. So they contain preservatives. Usually parabens, which it has been claimed are known toxic hazards.

We know that because there is now a plethora of creams out there claiming they don't contain them.

They usually contain synthetic fragrance, a level of petroleum by product and various other 'patent pending' ingredients that we can't talk much about because they are 'patent pending'.

As a matter of truth, the large commercial companies are more interested in their bottom line, than your health.

So please don't be naive and think otherwise. Just be aware.

By law, the cosmetic industry can make all manner of claims, and not have to prove any of them. They are self-regulating.

**What I have found over the years is that the real truth is so profoundly disturbing, that women refuse to hear it. They just switch off.**

The advertising and packaging is so persuasive, suggestive and seductive that it's never questioned.

Ever.

And the ramifications so great that we don't believe that anyone could be that blatantly underhand.

So I am simply going to pose two questions.

**If all the claims they stated are true, then why are we all not wrinkle free?**

**And if all the ingredients are so new, revolutionary and patent pending free, then who determines whether they will be safe to use on my skin for the next five years?**

> Your ego wants you to be 'pure'. And 'organic' and 'I've got more pebbles in my spa' natural than any other. Because it makes you appear spiritual and more intelligent than others. And just that little tad superior.

Oh, and another one...

**And who oversees the cumulative effect these patent pending ingredients have on my body, over time, when combined with the patent pending ingredients in my haircare, deodorant, perfume, eye cream, sunscreen and fake tan?**

Oh well...oops, let's move on.

A bit close to the bone that one.

Please feel free to skip this chapter if you really would like to, because we are now moving to your favourite topic...natural and organic...and you might be a little ruffled here too.

**Natural is not what you think. Natural can mean anything. So we can get away with a lot.**

And just because something is natural doesn't mean we can't add non-natural other ingredients too. And just because it is natural does not mean it contains the highest quality ingredients.

We know of one brand that used the beeswax candle shavings off the factory floor to put into its very expensive natural lip balm.

Which leads me to 'organic'. Currently **'organic' simply means anything that is comprised of a carbon chain.** That is all. It is not necessarily an indication something is pure. What does pure mean anyway?

**Your ego wants you to be 'pure'. And 'organic' and 'I've got more pebbles in my spa' natural than any other. Because it makes you appear spiritual and more intelligent than others. And just that little tad superior.**

Oh, the ego is tricky.

We had a shop for ten years in a beautiful tourist destination. An apothecary by the sea. Very often well to do women would come in and peer over their sunglasses at me, and ask, 'Yes, but is it ORGANIC?'

**In nine times out of ten, organic is just a marketing tool. It means nothing.**

My husband would roll his eyes, go to the back of the shop, and leave me with them. He just gave up.

**I am not advocating all organic skin care is so. Some are brilliant. They follow through and pay expensive due diligence. They forward think, and educate. They are increasingly on the rise.**

**But in fairness to those who tell the truth, be aware of those who don't.**

And ask your body. Yes, please remember your body.
And then there are perfumes.

**It takes many millions of dollars to launch a brand perfume worldwide.**

All commercial perfumes contain synthetic ingredients. They are no longer made in the traditional way. They contain synthetic copies of flowers, not the real thing. It is simply because there are not enough ingredients to go around. And it would just be too expensive anyway. Real absolutes are way more expensive than gold. And blending a natural perfume is an art form languishing in the too hard box. It's tricky dancing with Nature.

So the actual cost of the ingredients of some perfumes may amount to little more than a few cents a bottle. But the marketing and promotional budget as I mentioned is a different story.

Now I am an optimist.

I do believe that somewhere, someone will tell me the truth. So I recently tested my theory in one of our upmarket department stores here in Australia.

A new perfume had just been released. It was very expensive, very desirable, wonderfully marketed, and a gorgeously bottled, international brand.

Its marketing spiel sported all sorts of glorious floral ingredients.

I asked to sample some on a paper stick. I then asked the well-coiffed sales assistant what was in it. She told me the names of all sorts of flowers.

I picked up the box, and read the ingredients in front of her. There were none that she had mentioned, written on the box.

So I quietly showed her the list. There were no floral absolutes of natural extraction in the perfume.

But there was a list of chemical ingredients which mimicked them.

> *All commercial perfumes contain synthetic ingredients. They are no longer made in the traditional way. They contain synthetic copies of flowers, not the real thing. It is simply because there are not enough ingredients to go around. And it would just be too expensive anyway. Real absolutes are way more expensive than gold. And blending a natural perfume is an art form languishing in the too hard box. It's tricky dancing with Nature.*

What happened next was not surprising I guess, but suffice to say it was better that I left rather quickly. Her foot was shuffling uncomfortably, her nostrils were glaring and her fingernails were tapping on the counter. 'Lovely box,' I muttered, smiled and left.

**She had not told the truth. And she felt very uncomfortable.**

**Angry in fact.**

Now, I know it is not her fault, she was just repeating what she was told, but in effect, she lied to me. And tried to hide it.

And I caught her in the act.

**But here is the rub. Women have been led to believe that the industry cares about your health.**

**Some might. Most don't. It is up to you to equip yourself with the knowledge, and awareness to ask the difference.**

**Just what are you applying on your skin?**

And if you react, can you really sue? Because maybe it was just one of the many other ingredients you have applied to your skin for the last thirty years that caused the reaction? Who will prove what, when your body's tolerance reaches pussy's bow?

And how many people report reactions anyway? We usually blame ourselves.

It is our fault we are so sensitive, we say.

As more money goes down the beauty drain.

**But now you have the ultimate tool.**

# ASK YOUR BODY...right there in the store.

Just ask it. Next time you want to buy a face cream, night cream, throat cream, face serum, cleansing toner, anti-aging booster, deluxe smoother, radiant exfoliant, cellulite skin de-stressor,
or gloriously bottled perfume, just ask your body.

Hold the product next to your body, and ask it.

**Ask it. 'Body do you want me to apply this on you?'**

Let it lean forward for yes, or back for no. It is as simple as that.

**And do it, 'without a point of view'.**

You do not have to know all the names of the ingredients anymore. Your body doesn't care what the names are. It simply knows whether those ingredients are nurturing, nourishing, expansive for it, or not.

But, just for fun, read the labels anyway. You'll be surprised what you find.

Or don't find.

## Chapter Forty Four:

# The future can look rosy.

And what about me? How long have I been hanging out in the beauty bad lands, with nowhere to go? No one to talk to?

Well, I'm OK. I do quite nicely actually.

As providence has turned out, I get mine made for me. From the world's best roses.

In fact, we both do. **He has his roses, and I have mine.**

> *See, the energetic profile of Rose Damascena is self-acceptance.*
>
> *Just stick your head in a bunch of REAL roses and FEEL how good you feel!*
>
> *Yes, Heaven does have a smell.*

And both are bringing Heaven to Earth.

**See, the energetic profile of Rose Damascena is self-acceptance.**

**Just stick your head in a bunch of REAL roses and FEEL how good you feel!**

**Yes, Heaven does have a smell.**

**And when you wear rose absolute every day for nearly two decades, you cannot NOT accept who you really are.**

So I've had a little help to get here along the way.

I also have a wardrobe of body oils and perfumes made for my body.

All without a patent pending chemical in sight.

And nowhere on our packaging, nor website, nor message will you find an anti-wrinkle claim. I find it belittling. For someone else to

claim they can make me more beautiful. Especially with their patent pending cocktail.

**For we think you really are gorgeous, just the way you are.**

Sigh.

And pause.

Now I can hear you thinking, aren't there lots of natural creams out there? Some with roses, some with not. But all claiming pure essential oils, plant extracts, and alchemic wonders?

Yes, there are.

The aromatherapy world is another minefield, in fact, a more insidious one than you ever imagined.

For you would never know. You are not the expert, so the industry will inform you of what it wants you to hear, wants you to buy. And use a little poetic license along the way.

That is why we are creating a new generation of skin care and perfumes. It's called 'limited edition, ultra-natural, high frequency'. No spin, no compromise.

You see, we are now over it. Over the falsehoods, the shadows, the flagrant claims.

**Because your bodies are getting sick. Sick with chemical overload, sick with the lies.**

So I want to throw out a challenge, as part of this Gorgeous Revolution.

We can change all of this, one brand at a time.

We have to let them know our refined, now highly vibrating bodies require something different.

Test them. Test them with your new best friend, your body.

And don't buy if your body says no.

But demand now, something different.

As a skin care brand, we are a tiny little voice. There have been others before us, but this will knock your socks off too. They have mostly sold out.

They sell out to bigger brands for millions of dollars. The big brands change the formulations and the ingredients, and then trade off the former glory of the natural brand. Only they are not so natural any more.

You buy one of their products you have used for years, react to it, then blame yourself. The brand moves on, gathering less sensitive souls than you, and all is well.

We, dear readers, are the canaries in the coal mine. It is our highly vibrating bodies that are warning the others of what might come.

To my knowledge, I can only wear one skin care. My body rejects all others. I am physically ill with some brands, and have to wash vigorously should they get on my skin.

**So where does this lead us?**

> But the high vibrating naturals, the 100% Pure & Naturals, are different. The body feeds off them. It uses them in a synergistic way that is quite extraordinary. They literally energise the body and assist the healing process from the inside out.
>
> They complement our beings. They work to expand us, not contract us, to keep us well, not make us sick.

To a good place, I hope. But only if we now have a collective voice.

What I hope is this.

**That we start asking our bodies what they really want to have rubbed all over them.**

Give them the choice.
Ask them.

Our bodies are plant like. We are, after all, one with Nature.

We assimilate the genuinely natural world way better than the synthetic. We have to store the inert synthetic in our livers.
But the high vibrating naturals, the 100% Pure & Naturals, are different.

The body feeds off them. It uses them in a synergistic way that is quite extraordinary. They literally energise the body and assist the healing process from the inside out.

They complement our beings. They work to expand us, not contract us, to keep us well, not make us sick.

So with our grass roots, collective Gorgeous Revolutionary voices, we can drive the change we can now see possible.

**Now you know.**

**Now you can ask YOUR body and see, amongst the plethora of brands out there, just which one will work for you.**

And we ask those who want our oils and creams to ask their bodies too. For they are not for everyone. We must not have a point of view. Your body makes the choice, not your swayed, desiring mind.

Remember, your body makes the choice, not you.

Now there will HAVE to be change. Because if you don't buy their products, they will eventually have to ask why. And you can tell them.

**Because they are not vibrationally complementary with me.**

So, what would need to happen for that to change?

**What would it take for the industry to put your health, and your children's health, before its bottom line?**

And what would it take for more plants to be planted, higher standards of true purity to be applied, and ultra-natural smaller brands to flourish, ones that nourish and care for the planet, as well?

And all without a 'patent pending' claim in sight.

I wonder. I wonder.

THE GORGEOUS REVOLUTION

THE GORGEOUS REVOLUTION

## Chapter Forty Five:

## Generation G

**Gorgeous starts with 'G'.**

**So does 'Generosity of Spirit, Gratitude, Grace, Graciousness, Genius, Grey hair, Generative, and Giving'.**

Being gorgeous has nothing to do with looks. It is a word we spontaneously use to describe something delicious that creeps up on us and takes our breath away.

Children are gorgeous.
So are puppies, babies, big brie cheeses, plump plum tarts, full frocks, bunches of overblown roses, Turkish delight, dragon flies, ripe pomegranates,
light beams, luscious oils, beautiful sunsets, and handmade bread.
And some Italian men.

*This Gorgeous Revolution seeks women and men who want to live their lives with a Generosity of Spirit that opens the door for others, as well as themselves.*

Gorgeous has nothing to do with hard edges, closed hearts, green jealousies, or back stabbing nastiness.

**It has everything to do with LOVE.**

When we first introduced our rose cream in our shop, women would inhale gently, smile and say, that's gorgeous.

**So we named it Gorgeous Over Thirty Bunches Of Real Roses In A Jar Double Blended Cream.**

When our Hong Kong agent first opened a jar, she simple said, 'It made me feel happy'.

Well, it is time to be even more than happy.

**It is time to be Great. And Generous. And Generative.**

Greater than you've ever been prepared to be.

And big hearted Generous.

Generous with your gifts, your care, your kindness. Your strength. Your wisdom.

Your talents.

And Generative. Yes, you can generate the change you now want to see in this world.

**This Gorgeous Revolution seeks women and men who want to live their lives with a Generosity of Spirit that opens the door for others, as well as themselves.**

That opens the door for the Universe to engage in the gift of giving.

**For the universe is truly a generous place. Ask, and it is given.**

And to experience true giving, one must be willing to RECEIVE. It is reciprocal. You cannot have one without the other.

**And Generosity of Spirit is about being happy when others are happy.**

Finding joy in others' success, celebrating when life lands in each other's lap.

**Genuine Generosity of Spirit can only exist when we no longer are compelled to compete.**

**And the holy grail of external beauty keeps competition in place. Like glue.**

**So how to let go?**

**Gratitude.** Gratitude is gracious. Being grateful is the highest state one can be. It opens the heart, connects with all that is, and puts you in the flow of gifts.

Of evolutionary life itself.

It opens the door to receiving.

**Gratitude means saying thanks. For the air we breathe, for the voice we have, the food we eat, the friends we have, the family we love. The bigness we truly be.**

**The good times, and the bad. For it ALL has its place.**

It is the quickest, most potent way to turn our lives around.

**Be grateful, and all else falls away.**

Ask, every day.

> GRATITUDE will transform everything. Everything. Embrace it ALL.
>
> GRATITUDE is an energy. We can feel its truth. It is quiet. And deep.

**What's good about my talents I'm not prepared to see?**

**What's good about this situation I'm not prepared to see?**

**What's good about my body I'm not prepared to see?**

And focus on that. That which is good, that which rings right, that which is true and beautiful.

For everywhere there is love, even in the darkest of places.

**GRATITUDE will transform everything. Everything. Embrace it ALL.**

And please don't be this 'sickly sweet, spiritually significant, gratingly grateful' sycophant either. Because we all see through you.

**GRATITUDE is an energy. We can feel its truth. It is quiet. And deep.**

**And be GRACIOUS. Please say thank you. Look people in their eyes. Connect.**

**Do not rush through life. Be present. Take your time. Turn off your smart phone and take your time.**

I knew a woman once who folded her socks with **GRACE.** She folded mine once when she minded our children. She cared for each minute detail in life like it mattered.

She taught me how to bake bread, fold socks. I have not been able to duplicate her still presence, nor quiet order as yet, but give me time. I will surrender to the quietest movements of everyday living. The daily chores that reveal their gems.

For **GRACE** exists in the quiet breath of the moment. And we must listen to hear its whisper.

And **GENIUS**. Oh, yes genius. We all have it, but it must be released.

Dr John Demartini taught me a valuable habit. Every day, simply say,

**"I am a genius, and I apply my wisdom."**

When we do that, we truly get out of our own way and let the genius of The Universe come through. And we are brilliant beyond our humanly capacity. We become the thoughts, the eyes, the ears, the voice, and the heart of God.

Imagine, just for a moment, if we taught all our children that. All their genius, in all its forms, would blossom. Without an educational bell curve in sight.

**And grey hair. Ha. The GREY hair.**

What is it with grey hair? Ah, I remember now.

It was easy at first to cover The Grey. Then it started to peep out at the sides. Pop up more often, and make a nuisance of itself. I endured the colour, the chemicals, the smell. I endured it all, so I could pretend I was in control of this aging, I still looked young for my age and proud of my shiny dark hair.

Then, one day my hairdresser looked me square in the eyes, and told me:

**"GET over yourself."**

And I did. Just like that.

Julie, if you are reading this. I'm grateful.

But none of my 'girlfriends' spoke to me. Not one. I felt like the grey-haired elephant in the room. Not one had the courage to say, thank you. Thank you for breaking the mold, letting us all off the hook.

> *Nobody knows what to say. For when a woman goes Grey, she breaks ranks. She breaks rules.*

I watched my mother and other women her age battle with the colour bottle. Never wanting to give in. Because when you do, everyone will know you are getting old.

Even my grandmother had a bottle of hair colour in her drawer when she died at 83.

**Nobody knows what to say. For when a woman goes Grey, she breaks ranks. She breaks rules.**

She lets the side down.

The small side that is.

**But not the Bigger We.**

**So I am here to tell you the same.**

**It's OK. It's a choice. And, if you are ready, then**

**GET OVER YOURSELF!**

**Get a short cut. A GREAT cut.**

**And stop covering the grey. I dare you. Double dare you.**

Finger dry your hair and nourish it with coconut, jasmine, lemon verbena and ylang ylang.

**Throw out your dye (ever noticed it says poison on the box?), get a great pair of earrings, and get over yourself.**

And with the money you save, experiment with makeup. Try natural minerals, and soften your look.

Or darken your lipstick. Be daring. Be different.

Wear a hat. I don't care. Please just get over yourself.

**Be GENERATIVE. Be open to receiving energy and generating new ideas.**

**For that is what you are, nothing less than a giant generator.**

**A giant fractal with fresh ideas, more connections and an infinite array of choice.**

And keep moving.

**Keep quietly asking Where Am I Needed Today?**

Expand, grow, and be willing to change. In a heartbeat.

**For there is only now.**

What more can we be, what more can we receive, what more can we GENERATE here on the earth for the benefit of all?

And last, but not least…

## How can we GIVE?

I have a plan. I have a dream.

Our Gorgeous Revolution is about breaking the addiction we have to external beauty and finding a bigger joy.

A larger connection.

**Giving is a bigger joy.**

# THE GORGEOUS REVOLUTION

Imagine if just 1% of ALL money spent on beauty in the world, think dieting, cosmetic surgery, hair, teeth whitening, make up, anti-aging, spas, waxing, lasers, liposuction, facials, manicures, hair dyes and breast implants and more, could be given back.

It would be billions. Billions of dollars, changing millions of lives. Ours included.

To educate, micro finance local enterprise, provide sound water solutions, feed children, provide housing, healing, stop sex slavery, genital mutilation, blindness, cleft palates. And more.

And what if every day you felt down, you could give instead of buy, give instead of cry, and give instead of whinge.

What sort of no brainer is that?

**Giving opens your heart. Literally. I don't mean it in a stereotyped, metaphysical way, I mean really. Practically.**

Feel it.

Give someone a hug, a gift, a flower, a kind gesture, and see how you feel.

**Genuine Giving is Oneness in action.** Giving will heal the planet. But only when receiving comes with it.

> *Giving opens your heart. Literally. I don't mean it in a stereotyped, metaphysical way, I mean really. Practically.*

For the two are one.

**When you give, you receive you.**

The gift is in the giving. We all know that.

**Oh, and I just want to add a little secret here. Just a little one.**

At the beginning of the book, I say you won't find angels on the cover, anywhere.

I white-lied. Angels are everywhere. I know. Because I am one.

When my world caved in a few years ago, I chose to expand.

To surrender. To fly.

And I literally grew wings.

Big white ones.

It took four hours to birth and unfurl them, and an hour sitting in the sun to dry them. Like a big white cormorant.

I know. They are big, white and they are there.

And we all have them. Yours are waiting to unfurl too.

**When you jump.**

## Chapter Forty Six:

## Begin It Now.

If we don't change our global point of view, we will die. We will blow ourselves up, run out of room, poison the earth, and deplete all the soil, and compete 'til we die.

We will hate ourselves to a toxic death.

But if we are willing to change, anything is possible.

**But YOU must choose.**

**For it is you, as one with consciousness itself, who can be the change we are waiting for.**

I recently saw a well know star on TV. She was approaching seventy.

She looked thirty-five.

Her hair was perfectly coiffed, her teeth sparkled, her limbs were long and firm, her forehead was still and smooth. Her breasts were full, her waist small, her hands perfectly manicured and poised.

High maintenance, honey.

She was put forward as an example of ageless beauty.
What's wrong with that you ask?

Her heart was closed. She acted as if. She spoke of enlightenment. Of being in the light.

But her heart was closed. There was not an ounce of generosity in her beautiful, bountiful frame. Just lack.

Her vitality was fake. She wore a mask. Albeit it a beautiful one.

**I will pose you this.**

If we are to be here in one hundred years, we have to change what we see as beauty.

A radiance way beyond imagining awaits us all. And you cannot buy it in a jar. Nor get it from a laser.

To embrace the sage, the wise, the far flung ebullience that comes with wisdom and generosity that liberate the soul.

For they are there.

To celebrate those amongst us whose radiance comes from a deeper place. A bigger place we all know, but are sometimes afraid to be. And we must wake up and be that now. Whatever our age.

All over the planet. There is safety in numbers now.

> *For humanity to thrive, we must see beyond the botoxed brow, beyond the perfect breast, and see to the biggest heart of the matter.*
>
> *To our infinite selves.*
>
> *Our Bigger We.*

We must be that for our daughters, our sons, our husbands, our lovers, for ourselves.

**For humanity to thrive, we must see beyond the botoxed brow, beyond the perfect breast, and see to the biggest heart of the matter.**

**To our infinite selves.**

**Our Bigger We.**

**I invite you to join us now. Stop playing it small, start questioning now. And welcome to The Revolution. Our Doorway to Sovereignty.**

**Our Gorgeous Revolution.**

**Your time starts NOW.**

## Acknowledgements

The words in this book may have been written freely and quickly but its publishing has been another story. So, thank you to my close family and friends, for their faith that one day, yes, one day, my words will manifest. And yes, they have.

To Clive, my husband, who has made me a more robust, formidable and brave partner; to Dom, our daughter who has made me a more open, resilient, flexible and full mother, and to Benjamin, our son who has made me a softer version of me. I thank you.

To Moira my dear friend who has steadfastly seen in me what I see in her, and to my dog Speedo, who although no longer on this earth plane, taught me to love, again and again and again, no matter what.

To Cherilyn and her beautiful clothes and her invitation to be photographed by the genius of Steffen Boettcher, an experience we will all remember with the warmest of smiles.

To Michelle who initiated the editing and promotion, to gorgeous Dhana for her forensic eye and to Sean, who sat diligently with me to bring the words to life on the page. With bees.

And to the rest of my team. Thank you.
You know who you are.

## About the Author

Dee Light grew up in Melbourne in a middle-class way. A good girl from a nice family, she promptly swam the other way at the age of twenty- five and has robustly been following her own inner compass for over nearly four decades.

She didn't ask to write this book, it arrived and has occupied her psyche ever since.

Her favourite saying, 'When in deep water become a diver" means she delves, bringing up the crud we all want to hide. About how we feel about our bodies, our small lives, our relationships, our wobbly thighs and our big, private dreams.

The author gratefully acknowledges the contribution from:

**"To Love Yourself"** page 47
© em claire
All Rights Reserved
www.emclairepoet.com
printed with permission

**Photography:**
Steffen Boettcher
www.steffenboettcher.com
www.stilpirat.de

**Apparel:**
Zephyr Lounge Wear
www.zephyrloungewear.com

**Skincare and perfume:**
Manifesto of Light
www.manifestooflight.com

**Layout and Design:**
Sean Pascoe
seanpascoe@optusnet.com.au

**Printed by:**
Paradigm Print Media
www.paradigmprintmedia.com.au

**Published by:**
Deirdre Light 2017

ISBN number -13  978-0-6481223-0-2
ISBN number -10  0-6481223-0-1


copyright © Deirdre Light 2017

The moral right of the author has been asserted. All rights reserved.
No part of this publication may be reproduced, stored in a retrieval system, or transmitted, in any form or by any means, without the prior permission in writing of the publisher, nor be otherwise circulated in any form of binding or cover other than in which it is published and without similar condition including this condition being imposed on the subsequent purchaser.


Printed in Singapore